Surviving
the Storm

Surviving the Storm

*Finding God in the
Midst of a Marriage Breakdown*

Wendy Foxhall

Sovereign World

Sovereign World Ltd
PO Box 777
Tonbridge
Kent TN11 0ZS
England

ISBN 1 85240 395 0

The publishers aim to produce books which will help to extend and build up the Kingdom of God. We do not necessarily agree with every view expressed by the author, or with every interpretation of Scripture expressed. We expect each reader to make his/her judgement in the light of their own understanding of God's Word and in an attitude of Christian love and fellowship.

Cover design by CCD, www.ccdgroup.co.uk
Typeset by CRB Associates, Reepham, Norfolk
Printed in the United States of America

Dedication

*This book is dedicated to my children, Joanna and Tom –
the most caring, talented, cleverest, funniest, wonderfully
unique, special, totally amazing children
that any mum could wish for.*

Contents

Acknowledgments

A huge, huge 'thank you' to my lovely friends who listened endlessly and patiently to me wittering on. To Steve and Debbie – thanks Deb for being such a wonderful, loyal, caring friend, for the many hours spent at my kitchen table listening, and for not minding when I crashed your new car. Thanks Steve for feeding the cats and for being available when I needed someone to change the taps. Thanks to Linda and Tony, Rena, Lucy and Annie for being there when I needed you. Thanks Barbara for your support and encouragement, and to Andrew for your wisdom, and for making me laugh. To Jane, for garden centres, cups of tea and slices of cake. Thanks to Alwyn, you're a star. To Julie in the US (the long-suffering recipient of many midnight emails), and to my lovely counsellor Rosemary. Thank to Gisela who, going through the same experience at the same time, was able to provide sympathy and understanding. Thanks also to Nick, who encouraged me to write this book. And last but not least, thanks to Tim Pettingale, my publisher, for liking my book enough to publish it.

'... *they are no longer two individuals: they are one flesh.*
What God has joined together, man must not separate.'

(Mark 10:8–9, RSV)

I found Marcel alone

It was about noon when I knocked at his door.
I found Marcel alone, still lying on the bed which was now too big
    for him;
His wife left him a few days ago.

It hurt me, Lord, to see that poor fellow so discouraged, that house
    half-empty.
A presence was lacking.
A love was lacking.
I missed the bunch of flowers on the mantelpiece, the powder and
      lipstick on the wash-basin, the scarf on the bureau and the
      chairs properly arranged.
I found the sheets dirty on a bed wrinkled like an old face,
      the ash-trays filled to overflowing, shoes scattered on the floor,
      a rag on the easy-chair, and the blinds closed.
It was dark, dismal and stuffy.

It hurt me, Lord.
I felt something torn,
   something unbalanced,
Like a mechanism gone wrong,
Like a man with broken bones.

And I reflected that what you had planned was good,
And that there can be no order and beauty, love and joy, outside of
    your plan.

I pray to you tonight, Lord,
   for Marcel and for her
   and for the other one
   and for the wife of the other one
   and for his children
   and for the families involved
   and for the neighbours who gossip
   and for the colleagues who judge.

I ask of you forgiveness
   for all these lacerations,
   for all these wounds

and for your blood poured out, because of these wounds,
in your Mystical Body.
I pray to you tonight, Lord, for myself and for all my friends.
Teach us to love.

It is not easy to love, son.
Often when you think you love, it is only yourself that you love,
and you spoil everything, you shatter everything.

To love is to meet oneself, and to meet oneself one must be willing
to leave oneself and go towards another.
To love is to commune, and to commune one must forget oneself for
another,
One must die to self completely for another.
To love hurts, you know, son,
For since the Fall – listen carefully, son – to love is to crucify oneself
for another.

(Michel Quoist)[1]

Chapter 1

The Storm

*'Without warning, a furious storm came up on the lake,
so that the waves swept over the boat.
But Jesus was sleeping.'*
(Matthew 8:24)

Storms have a habit of doing that, arriving without warning and catching us unawares. One minute we're sailing along under a cloudless blue sky, waves lapping gently against the sides of the boat and everything is right with the world. The next moment the sky is angry and grey, the wind has risen, torrential rain is lashing down and the boat is swaying out of control. Without any warning whatsoever, the storm clouds broke one gloriously sunny Good Friday morning when my twenty-nine-year marriage came to an abrupt end. My husband had left me, a friend had left her husband (the two incidents were connected), and in the course of one day, two families were broken; two sets of lives were shattered and changed forever.

During the weeks and the months that followed, with the storm raging around me, it seemed as though Jesus really was asleep in the boat. I called out to Him over and over. Sometimes He answered me, sometimes I could feel His presence, but more often than not, I saw Him in the distance, arms folded, just out of hearing and waiting to see what I would do, how I would react, leaving me to my own devices.

'How long, O Lᴏʀᴅ? Will you forget me forever?
  How long will you hide your face from me?
  How long must I wrestle with my thoughts
    and every day have sorrow in my heart?
  How long will my enemy triumph over me?'

(Psalm 13:1–2)

There are times in our life when God seems far away, when we call out to Him and our cries appear to go unheard; when He seems not to care and when, from time to time, we may even wonder if there is a God. We have only to read through the Psalms to realise that we are not alone in this and that it is okay to doubt. We will question, we will cry out, we will earnestly pray, we will ask, 'Why Lord?' And we are answered by silence. God seems indifferent.

That's how it seemed at the time and yet, looking back, I can now see that He was there all the time.

Folk Tale
Prayers like gravel
Flung at the sky's
window, hoping to attract
the loved one's
attention. But without
visible plaits to let
down for the believer
to climb up,
to what purpose open
that far casement?
I would
have refrained long since
but that peering once
through my locked fingers
I thought that I detected
the movement of a curtain.   (R.S. Thomas)[2]

Instinctively we cry out to God, like a child who wakes in the night from a bad dream and calls for his parents. Somehow or other, in spite of seeming evidence to the contrary, and simply because there really is no option, we have to keep on believing that God is in control in the midst of all the mess, even when it seems as though our prayers are floating off unheard into an empty void.

Disaster can strike any day, at any time. We have no control over our future. None of us knows in advance when the storm will break. We like to think we have our future planned and mapped out, but in reality, none of us can be sure of what tomorrow will bring. We can plan for it, pay into our pension policies, plan for our retirement, buy a nice house, save money, and take out insurance policies. But in reality, none of us know, *really* know, what's going to happen in the next hour, never mind tomorrow or next year. Change can come in a moment, and our whole future as we've planned it can be wiped out. The only person who knows our future is God. Ultimately, we need not put our hope in things, not in the money we accumulate in the bank, not in our pension or insurance policies, not in our nice houses or retirement plans, and not in human relationships, but in God.

Some things in this life are certain; we are born, we die, and somewhere along the journey from one point to the other, we will all hit stormy waters. This book is intended for those who are, at this moment, standing unsteadily in the rocking boat with the wind howling mercilessly and the waves crashing around them – those people who have had their security taken away from them, who thought they knew where they were going, but somehow or other, have lost their bearings and mislaid the map; they are alone in the dark, afraid and disorientated, with the storm raging around them.

This can happen at any stage of life and in various ways: the death of a loved one, illness, bankruptcy, redundancy, marriage breakdown and divorce. It is these last two that are the subject of this book. Although many of the emotions, reactions and coping mechanisms are common to all these forms of calamity, marriage breakdown and divorce carry their own particular torture and pain.

We'd all like to believe that Christian marriages survive and the vast majority do, but we are all human beings with human frailties. As Christians we are subject to the same temptations and tensions as everyone else. Some make it, some don't. Research carried out in 1999 by the Barna Research Group in the US demonstrated the alarming fact that not only is divorce happening among Christians, but that it is even more prevalent than among those who are non-Christians. Using statistics drawn from a US nationwide survey in 1999 involving nearly 4,000 adults, 27% of born-again Christians are currently, or have previously been, divorced, compared to 24% in the rest of the population.[3]

These surprising statistics beg the question of whether churches are providing the necessary support to help couples stay together during marital crisis. Perhaps many couples are afraid to be honest about their problems for fear of being perceived as failures, for fear of being lectured and told the error of their ways, for fear of not being treated with compassion, understanding and grace. How many couples have reached out to their church for help but have not received what they were hoping for, maybe because of a lack of experienced counsellors, or maybe because of a 'bury your head in the sand – this doesn't happen to Christians' attitude? How many couples in the average congregation attend church every Sunday, sitting together in the pews and presenting to the world the picture of the perfect Christian marriage, whilst the reality is somewhat different?

The Bible tells us that God always brings good things out of bad experiences. If you had explained to me in advance what was about to happen to me, if you had told me about the almost unendurable pain, the loss of confidence, the rejection, the loneliness, the regret, anger and guilt, the hours spent weeping, the depression, the humiliation, the feelings of betrayal, the grief for a marriage I thought would last until death, the doubts about the goodness of God, and the fear of the future, I would not have thought I could survive it. But survive I did. Through crisis we discover the strength inside. Through this experience God has given me strength, demonstrated His wonderful, amazing grace and mercy to me in a tangible way, shown me things about myself that I didn't know were there, drawn me closer to Himself, and demonstrated over and over to me that I can safely place my future in His hands and that He continues daily to work out His purposes for me. God is an opportunist; He will take the failures, the crises in our lives, and use them to make us the kind of people He always intended us to be. I've learnt that when almost everything is taken away – in my case, my husband, my security, part of my identity, my plans for the future, some of my friends, and my home – there remains one thing and one thing only; one person – God. Unlike human beings, God will never disappoint us, never let us down or abandon us. Sometimes, the only way we can learn this truth is to go through the times of adversity and allow God to show us who He really is.

When any of us are faced with this kind of situation, we are also faced with a choice. The Chinese character for the word 'crisis' denotes both 'danger' and 'opportunity' and there is the potential to go either way. If we are to land safely on the side of opportunity, we need the support of friends, family, and the professionals: doctors, lawyers and counsellors. As Christians, we need the support of our church and, most importantly, a belief – no matter how tenuous at time – in the enduring love of God. We can go under and become a victim, or we can overcome and allow God to use the experience to make us into the kind of people He wants us to be. This means surrender and it's not easy. It means handing over the control of our lives to another, and that's always scary. The tendency is to want things back the way they were, to return to the familiar, but what's happened has happened and we can't undo the past. Somehow we must learn to let go of the past, trust our future to God, and learn to live in the moment, taking hold of whatever opportunities come our way.

There is a process to be worked through and it is very similar to the process of grief. In many ways it can be worse than grief, especially if we are the one who has been left behind, if our partner has left us for someone else. The pain can be excruciating, involving not only grief but also rejection and humiliation.

The end of a marriage, although incredibly sad and devastating, can be the start of something new, something exciting, causing us to take stock of our lives, reorder our priorities, find out who we are, and make changes. In the midst of the inevitable pain we still have a choice to make. We can be swamped by it, allowing it to cripple us and erode our confidence and self-esteem, or we can choose to view it as an opportunity. God will always bring good out of bad situations – providing we let Him.

What of those disciples in the boat with the storm raging around them? They panicked. They woke the sleeping Jesus and demanded that He do something. With a few words, He calmed the storm.

Everything seems to be out of control; your whole world appears to have crumbled and where is Jesus? He seems to be asleep. Unlike you, He's not scared. He knows that His Father is in control. Stick close to Him in the boat and with one word He can calm the storm. He knows that you will heal, become a fully functional human being and find joy once again.

> 'When you're faced with something that painful, you have two choices. You can go down, go under – just cave in out of the fear of what it means to be single again. Or you can say this is to open a door that I'd never even thought of opening.'   (Jane Fonda)[4]

Chapter 2

Shock

'What I feared has come upon me;
what I dreaded has happened to me.
I have no peace, no quietness;
I have no rest, but only turmoil.'
(Job 3:25–26)

Shock is a physical reaction to severe emotional trauma. Emotions are blocked; reactions and mental processes are affected and we do not react in normal, rational ways. I remember very little about that first weekend when my husband left me – shock does strange things to you. I remember that one of the first things I did was to clean the windows! It was mundane physical activity designed to stop me thinking, to prevent me absorbing the truth that, at that time, I was incapable of comprehending – that my husband of twenty-nine years was gone, and that my life would never be the same again. I went through that whole weekend on automatic, baking a cake, cooking for my adult children, who were home for the Easter weekend, and watching TV with them.

It's a terrifying thing to find yourself suddenly alone in the dark with an uncertain future ahead of you and during the coming months your emotions will be in turmoil. This is quite normal, if very unpleasant, and you are not going mad! You will come through and will emerge stronger and able to see all manner of possibilities that eluded you at the start.

That first night was a peculiar mixture of seeming to be asleep, yet being awake at the same time. My mind was conscious, teeming, with the adrenaline flowing. I must have drifted off at some point. I remember waking and thinking, 'This can't be happening, it's crazy.' I wrote in my journal,

> 'This has to be the single most bizarre thing that's ever happened to me. Like living on the set of a soap opera. I woke up this morning with the sun streaming through the curtains and the family all here, with one exception, and a family Easter weekend all planned, thinking, "this is total madness."'

It seemed so unreal, I could have expected my husband to turn up at any moment and announce that it had all been a sick joke.

Later on that day I wrote, 'However the circumstances might appear, however bad things might seem, God is in control.' I had to believe it. I had to.

Crying

I was forever bursting into tears. With friends, with family, in the car, in the house, out walking – the tears would pour uncontrollably down my face. Once I started it seemed as though I would never stop. I remember a train journey where I embarrassed myself by sitting in a carriage, helplessly weeping, surrounded by the other passengers who pretended not to have noticed.

That first weekend, I went to the supermarket with my children and burst into tears halfway round. For months I couldn't go into a supermarket without crying, without having a panic attack and wanting to put the basket down and run. For me, shopping was associated with caring, nurturing, loving. On one of my first shopping trips after my husband left, I found myself at the checkout with, among other things, a large carton of his favourite yoghurt. It sat in the fridge for weeks before I threw it away. For me, supermarket shopping was a reminder of meals lovingly cooked and shared. Then came the day when I realised that I could buy what *I* wanted to eat. I could buy *my* favourite food, things I hadn't included in the family menus for years because my husband didn't like them. That was quite a revelation for me.

I also couldn't bear to watch holiday programmes on TV. They brought back so many memories of happy holidays spent together or with the family.

Similarly, a song could reduce me to tears. I remember sitting in a bar with my son only a few weeks after my husband had left and hearing a particular song, a memory from the early years of my marriage. I was a blubbering wreck within seconds and sitting in this very public place with the tears steaming down my face, much to my son's embarrassment.

It's perfectly okay to cry; don't try to stop yourself, allow the tears to flow. It's important to experience the turmoil of emotion that will overwhelm you right now. There is a tendency for some people to think, 'I must be strong, I mustn't cry.' They try to pretend that everything is fine, that they are not hurting. They try to block out the pain, to keep going, to have a 'stiff upper lip', but suppressed emotions never remain suppressed. They emerge at some extremely inconvenient moment in the future and cause havoc to you and those who happen to be in the firing line.

Indulge your sadness if you can bear it, listen to sad songs, watch weepy movies with a box of tissues by your side, look at the photos, sit at a pavement café drinking coffee, watch the couples go by and feel sad. It's all a part of the process.

Obsessive thinking

Obsessive thinking is a feature of shock, and for months I thought about nothing else. I went to bed thinking about *it*, and I woke up thinking about *it*. I dreaded those moments between sleeping and waking, when the conscious mind begins to rise through the layers of sleep, and when the memory comes flooding back remorselessly. I would fight to go back to sleep, to sink back into that place of oblivion.

It was incredibly tiring, and for months my brain did not rest for a moment, going over and over the same old things – conducting imaginary conversations and writing letters to my husband in my head, trying to find a solution. I prayed that God would release me, and that I could think about something else. Gradually, as time goes on, you will find yourself thinking about it less and less. I promise!

Talking

I probably bored my friends rigid talking about it, but that talking, the almost uncontrollable spewing out of words, was essential to my healing. It was as though I had a huge collection of words; I threw them out in front of me and there they lay, all jumbled up. I picked them up and put them together, making sentences with them, trying to make sense of the situation, trying to come to terms with what had happened. I am so grateful for my friends and family, who listened endlessly and patiently to me saying the same things again and again. They, with their love and their patience and their willingness to listen, were a source of healing to me. Talk to trusted friends or seek counselling; grab every opportunity for healing. Choose your friends carefully though. In my case there were just two or three people that I knew I could trust. Avoid like the plague anyone who might have a tendency to gossip and to pass on to someone else the things you tell him or her.

Even in a church there is gossip. At first you will want to try and contain as much as possible in order to stem the inevitable tittle-tattle. This is perfectly okay. You can choose to tell as much or as little as you choose, to whosoever you choose.

By talking we process things and eventually come to terms with what has happened. Grab every opportunity that you can. If there are counsellors in your church, go to see them. I went to 'Relate' and found them very helpful indeed. The counsellors undergo rigorous training, and the great advantage of a professional organisation like Relate is that the counsellors are completely objective. They don't know you or your partner, and just their objectivity alone can sometimes help you to see things more clearly. Close friends are wonderful, but they maybe have a tendency to agree with everything you say and take your side completely; which is okay – that's what friends are for! But it helps the process if you get an objective viewpoint too. Primarily, the job of the counsellor is to listen, not to be judgmental, not to offer advice, and to help you come to terms with what has happened and find a way forward. The best thing we can do for a friend in turmoil is to listen. Just that. We don't need to offer advice – just be there to listen.

Exhaustion

Exhaustion, both physical and mental, is a feature of shock; all this emotional turmoil is very tiring. The most important thing to remember during this time is to have grace and compassion with yourself and to allow yourself a period of recuperation. Don't allow your own or other people's expectations to influence you; rest whenever you can, and take each day as it comes. If you don't feel like going out, don't go out. Recognise that you are not functioning normally and expect to go through a whole gamut of emotions, to feel differently one day to the next, or from one hour to the next; one moment feeling positive, maybe even euphoric, the next moment weeping uncontrollably, and feeling as though you have totally lost the plot. One moment feeling anger, the next, guilt. If it's a bad day, just go with it, and do whatever you have to do to get through the day. You don't need to feel guilty if you haven't done this or that, as it will wait until another day. The important thing just now is *you*, and your recovery. The process can take much longer than you want it to and shock can last for months. Have patience with yourself and expect it to take time.

Task management

On your good days, try to get essential tasks done. Sometimes, these can appear overwhelming. A good idea is to write down each task and break it down into smaller, more achievable units, ticking off each task as you go, and carrying the remainder over to the next day if necessary. Don't be too proud to ask for help with mundane tasks. Those offers of help are not just empty words. Sometimes people aren't quite sure how to help or what to say, and doing practical things allows them to reach out to you. People genuinely want to be of use, so don't be too proud to accept, and don't be too proud to ask for help either. Friends will be more than happy to come to your aid.

Prioritise – decide what is important and what needs to be done today, what can wait until tomorrow or next week, and what actually doesn't need doing at all. Nothing dreadful is going to happen if you don't mow the lawn today or if you don't buy Auntie Maureen a birthday present this year.

Be selfish for a while. Try to do things that you enjoy doing – gardening, playing sport, joining a gym, going for walks, whatever. I immersed myself in novels. While I was reading and being totally absorbed in the plot, of someone else's life (even if they were only fictional beings), I couldn't think about *It*.

During this stage you may not want to eat. I didn't. But it's essential that you try to eat regularly, and to eat the right foods. You need strength now, both physical and mental. This is your time for healing, so cherish yourself.

Writing as therapy

If you have the inclination, write a journal. I found this extremely helpful. The University of Texas recently carried out research and discovered the therapeutic benefits of writing about one's feelings, pouring them all out onto paper. Pour out your feelings. Make a note of scriptures, quotes you come across, anything. By writing down how you feel, you are processing the chaos in your head and making sense of it. A journal is a valuable outlet for the churning and seemingly uncontrollable emotions inside. You might never want to read it again, but it serves a very useful purpose. It is important to express your feelings; don't try to analyse, just let it all come tumbling out – the anger, the loneliness, the regrets, the despair, the terror and every other emotion that bombards you. You will find that as you begin to write, the thoughts and feelings will flow. Keep on writing until you feel that you've finished. Don't think, 'Oh, I can't do that, I can't write.' You're not writing a novel! It doesn't matter about punctuation or grammar. It doesn't have to be in your best handwriting. No one is going to give you marks out of ten for it. Assume that no one else will ever read it except you.

Don't feel that you have to write every day. Some days you may write in it two or three times, then a week will go by, or two weeks, or longer. This is not like one of those diaries that you had for Christmas as a child, where you diligently wrote in it every day, forgot to write in it somewhere around the middle of January, and then abandoned it altogether because you'd missed a few days.

It shouldn't be a description of events – the things you did that day or the people you met, along the lines of 'Went to supermarket then went to the doctors, then went to the Post Office'. The purpose of the exercise is to document your feelings, expose them, face them and deal with them.

Try to end each entry on a positive note; don't only fill it with the negative stuff. As you travel through the process of bereavement, it may be a good idea, at times, to read through your journal, if only to see how far you've progressed – to see that the feelings are no longer as intense and crippling as they were at the beginning. One day, you will read your journals and see them as a testimony to the healing process, to the way that God has brought you through. I can verify that keeping a 'feelings' journal is a sanity-saver. Write down your innermost thoughts and feelings, things you can't even tell your friends. Then hide it!

Pain avoidance

Try not to block out the pain with other things, like retail therapy or alcohol. Lots of shopping might make you feel better for a while – until the credit card statement arrives, giving you something else to worry about. Alcohol makes you feel worse and renders you less capable of handling day-to-day tasks. It will make you feel more depressed and serves no purpose other than to temporarily block out the pain, burying the feelings that are a necessary part of the healing process. It's something else to feel guilty about and erodes the sense of control you have over your life even more. Alcohol is a mood enhancer. If you are feeling low and depressed before you drink, you will feel even lower and more depressed after drinking. Likewise with eating – don't overindulge. That packet of chocolate biscuits may make you feel better for a very short time, but will do nothing for your already rock-bottom self-esteem when they turn up later, piled onto various parts of your anatomy.

Some people behave like teenagers with rampant hormones; they go out clubbing and dating as though there is no tomorrow. Others deal with the situation by going into overdrive. They fill their lives with work, activity and people in order to avoid having to face their incredibly painful emotions. This is not a good idea – not only will it sap you of your energy, but at some point in the future, those emotions will emerge and smack you in the face when you least expect it.

Loss of concentration

I would find myself forgetting what I was doing or saying, becoming distracted in the middle of a task. I would start to empty the wash basket and then wander off and do something else, returning to the bedroom some time later and wondering why the contents of the wash basket were all over the floor. I'd regularly forget where I'd parked the car after a shopping trip and would spend ages wandering up and down the rows of parked cars feeling very silly, pretending (in case anyone was watching) that I knew perfectly well where my car was. During conversation I would lose my thread mid-sentence. I wanted to talk to people, needed to talk to them, but the effort of concentration was almost too much, and my mind would go totally blank; the 'screen saver' would come down. I needed to concentrate very hard indeed to remember a sequence of events – who said what, and what happened afterwards.

Panic attacks

Often, I would go into town to do some shopping, only to find myself hurtling back to the safety of the car before a single purchase had been made. I couldn't stand crowds. It was as though this great mass of people had become huge and frightening. I had shrunk and become very small and vulnerable, and I would be desperate for the safety and sanctuary of my own home. This would happen in church, or even sometimes at a friend's house with a group of people.

If this happens to you, find somewhere quiet (if possible) and take some deep breaths. Pray; tell yourself that you are safe, that you can cope with the situation. Wait until you have calmed down, and then return. If you still feel panicky, go home. People will understand.

One step forward, two steps back

It's important to recognise that we do not progress through the stages of grief in an orderly fashion. For grief is what it is – we grieve for our partner as though they had died. And we grieve for a marriage that is over. God views us as dearly beloved and unique individuals, but when we marry we become one person. Genesis 2:24 says:

> 'For this reason a man will leave his father and mother and be united to his wife, and they will become one flesh.'

There is the husband, there is the wife and there is a third person – the marriage. Spiritually, to rip apart the relationship is to abort, to kill, that third person.

No wonder it is so painful. We may feel okay one day, seeming to accept the situation and being positive, looking forward to the future, but the following day we take two steps back and find ourselves being overwhelmed by those feelings we thought we'd left behind. This bewildering and unpleasant experience can go on for a very long time, much longer than we hope or expect. But it will get easier and less painful as time goes on.

I don't believe that time heals. Time allows us to assimilate the experience, allowing it to become a piece in the jigsaw, a part of the damaged individuals we all are. Time lessens the pain, but only God can heal.

The presence of God

The most important thing is to spend time with God. He is the One who comforts and heals. Try to find time to be alone with Him each day. Even if you can't feel His presence, and even if your prayers seem to be floating off into a big black hole, God hears them and He knows what you are going through. Psalm 139:1–6 says this:

> 'O LORD, you have searched me
>   and you know me.
> You know when I sit and when I rise;
>   you perceive my thoughts from afar.
> You discern my going out and my lying down;
>   you are familiar with all my ways.
> Before a word is on my tongue
>   you know it completely, O LORD.
> You hem me in – behind and before;
>   you have laid your hand upon me.
> Such knowledge is too wonderful for me,
>   too lofty to attain.'

God created you, He knows you better than you know yourself and He cares passionately about you and what you are experiencing. Through Jesus Christ, He understands your frailties and your human emotions. Don't be afraid to rant and rave, to get very angry, to question Him, to express the doubts and the fears – He knows all about them anyway. Just as you would express all this stuff to a very close friend, express it to God, for He is your very closest friend. For years I was very polite with God. I told Him only those things I thought that He would want to hear; I was on my best behaviour, as we would be with someone we don't know very well. But He knew that underneath the mask there was an ugly, messy, seething mess of emotions, questionable motives, doubts, and a profound lack of trust. God longs for us to be real, to be honest, to be human – He can cope with it. Only when we are honest with Him can he begin to deal with those things.

Realise that however out of control things might appear, God is in total command of your situation; He 'hems you in', has laid His hand upon you. If He is for you, who can be against you? He has a future for you and is not at all phased that the life plan seems to have gone awry. He will triumph in and through your life. Talk to Him, listen to Him, know that He has you firmly by the hand and will not let you go. Know also that this phase will come to an end; you won't always feel this way. Psalm 13 continues:

> *'But I trust in your unfailing love;*
> *my heart rejoices in your salvation.*
> *I will sing to the* Lord*,*
> *for he has been good to me.'* (Psalm 13:5–6)

He has been good to you in the past and He will be good to you in the present and in the future. He is Sovereign. We may not understand why this is happening to us but we must come to a place where we praise Him anyway, simply because He is God – not because of what He gives us and not just for His blessings – a place where we seek the Giver, not the gift. Where we must continue to trust Him, no matter what. Where we must lay down our desires and our will. Where we realise there is no other course of action, no other alternative, nowhere else to turn. Even if you don't feel like it, praise Him for who He is. Play worship CDs. Just the very act of filling your home or your car with worship and praise to God does something in your spirit, and changes the atmosphere.

And what of the scripture at the start of this chapter? What of Job and his fear and turmoil? Flicking to the last page in the story we read, *'The* LORD *blessed the latter part of Job's life more than the first'* (Job 42:12).

When dawn finally arrives there will be life in abundance waiting for you; He has things in store for you that you cannot imagine right now. Hang on in there. Things can only get better.

'Failures are but milestones on the road to success.'

(Italian proverb)

Checklist

- Understand that your emotions are in turmoil and that this is a perfectly normal and natural reaction.

- Realise that physically and mentally you are under par. Don't expect too much of yourself.

- Don't be too proud to ask for help.

- Nurture yourself.

- Try writing down your thoughts and feelings.

- Talk to trusted friends and family. Seek counselling.

- Spend time with God.

Chapter 3

Denial

*'There is a time for everything,
and a season for every activity under heaven.'*
(Ecclesiastes 3:1)

Denial follows closely on the heels of shock. Denial is a strange thing; it is the nature of it that we don't know that we are in denial. When a marriage comes to an end we feel as though we have been cut adrift – lost and afraid in the middle of the ocean, not knowing where we're going. We will probably feel confused and panic-stricken, and we may desperately try to avoid those terrifying feelings and cling onto hope; hope that he or she will come back, hope that the relationship will be restored, and hope that things will return to how they were, even if the marriage was an unhappy one. The truth of the matter is, that even if the marriage were put back together again, it would never be the same, and in all probability would not survive. We cling desperately with our fingernails onto something that will never, ever return, something that is gone forever, sad though it might be. There may be many people for whom the end of a profoundly unhappy marriage is a huge relief, as they may have been at the receiving end of physical or emotional abuse. However, such people are unlikely to be reading this book.

I wanted to wake up one morning and discover that it had all been a nightmare – an awful dream. For several months I couldn't come to terms with what had happened, and wanted to believe that my husband might come back. I wanted desperately to talk to him; maybe if I said the right things he'd see the light, understand and come back. Maybe if I prayed hard enough, if enough of my friends prayed enough and if we prayed the right prayers, then God would listen and bring him back.

A well-meaning friend lent me a Christian book. The message of the book was that we should never give up praying and waiting for our partner to come back. Even if he or she is living with someone else, we should behave in such a way that they will want to return. We should not get angry but should be compassionate and understanding instead. In my opinion, Hosea might have been able to do it but us lesser mortals find it somewhat difficult to put out the welcome mat, being all sweetness and light, saying nothing antagonistic and enquiring pleasantly after the other woman/man. I tried for a while, but it didn't work!

Running back

Our natural inclination is to want to return to what we know and to what feels safe. The alternative is an unknown future that we are not yet strong enough to face, a blank page. The ending of a marriage, especially one that has survived for many years, is incredibly painful. At this point in time we are unable to face reality and we will turn and try to blindly run back the way we came, back to our comfort zone, and clinging onto false hope.

Contact

So, how do we know we're in denial? If we are still hoping that the relationship will be restored in spite of all the evidence to the contrary, we haven't come to terms with what has happened. We try to initiate contact.

My downfall was email. I sent those 'what a horrible worm-like creature I am', 'please come back to me, I know it can work' emails. Had I sat down with a piece of paper and a pen, bought a stamp and had to walk to the post box, most of those very embarrassing letters wouldn't have been sent. A highly unbalanced and lonely woman, late at night with access to a computer, is a dangerous combination.

No matter how tempting it might be to make that phone call or send that letter, try not to do it. If the letter is ignored, or if it elicits a negative or hostile response, you will end up feeling worse. Write the letter, but put it away in a drawer, telling yourself that you might send it one day. You probably won't. Wean yourself away, one day at a time. At first this will be very hard to do, like an alcoholic battling with his addiction.

Life is unfair

At this very moment there will be someone, somewhere in the world, who hears the news that they have a terminal illness, someone who crosses the road never to reach the other side, or someone whose day begins with optimism and ends in tragedy. Life is unpredictable and calamity can come to us all; life is unfair. Jesus said, *'In this world you will have trouble. But take heart! I have overcome the world'* (John 16:33). Being a Christian does not make us exempt from trouble or from unfair things happening to us. Life just happens. The difference is that we have Jesus Christ, someone who feels our pain, who has borne our sins on the cross; someone who loves us to bits and wants to see us healed, to enjoy the kind of life He has in store for us. However, it's not always easy to see that in the midst of our pain.

My own situation seemed dreadfully unfair, and I felt as though there had been a *fait accompli*. I had not had the opportunity to discuss, argue, or say how I felt. I was simply presented with my husband's decision. After he'd gone, there were still so many things I wanted to say. I wanted to argue my corner as it seemed so grossly unfair. I would hold long, imaginary conversations with him in my head, conversations in which I always managed to get my point over, say all I wanted to say, and of course, he always understood my point of view!

How to pray

What do we pray? Do we pray for restoration of the marriage? God's heart is always for restoration, but ultimately He allows us free choice. Maybe the best thing to pray for is that God's will be done in your partner's life, and for justice to be done. I thought this was a rather harsh thing to pray until a friend pointed out to me that God's justice can, and does, include mercy.

I remember feeling that if I gave up praying for his return, I would have failed – that I needed to keep holding on, to keep praying, never to believe that it was over. It was very tiring. I almost felt as though it were all down to me and how much and how earnestly I prayed, and that I was in a battle in which I had to keep going. I remember one summer evening, sitting in an armchair becoming aware of a wasp crashing over and over into a window frame, trying to get out. I remember thinking that if the wasp changed its position just a couple of inches to the left it could escape. I suddenly realised that I was like that wasp, crashing over and over again into the pane of glass and exhausting myself in the process. I needed to change position, move out of the way and allow God to work. I was trying to do His work by striving. It was at that moment that I knew I had to hand it all over to Him and pray, 'Not my will, but your will be done.'

Denying it's over

My husband didn't help by refusing to say that it was over and he continued to visit for some months. When asked the question, he'd refuse to say that he wouldn't come back. Instead he'd say, 'I don't know.' He came round every weekend to mow the lawn, to see if there was any post, to collect something from the house, and to visit my children when they were home. He occasionally popped in at lunchtimes, on some pretext or other. On several occasions he would hug me and kiss me on the cheek. Some couples still have sex together, despite the fact that they are separated and maybe living with other people.

During this time I would live from visit to visit, making sure I looked my best, ensuring that the house was tidy and cared for (I wanted him to look around and realise what he had given up!). He even took me out for dinner twice during the first few weeks. These were extremely bizarre occasions. Being with him in a restaurant was so familiar that we would find ourselves chatting about the children and work, and for a few minutes it would appear as though everything was as it used to be. It almost seemed as though we would get into the car and go home together.

Although the one who leaves has probably thought about it for a while, and will quite likely have been through part of the grieving process before they leave, they still find it difficult to accept that the relationship is well and truly over, and they may keep returning under one pretext or another. They are in shock and denial too, even if they are in a relationship with someone else. Where this happens, and the couple continue to see each other, the process will take much longer. Sometimes, especially if young children are involved, it's very difficult to avoid contact, but try to keep it to a minimum. You can't feel anger while there's still hope, and anger is a necessary part of healing.

Rose-tinted spectacles

During this phase, people will idealise their relationship and their former partner. The husband who used to sit in front of the TV all night and grunt occasionally, metamorphoses into someone with a fascinating line in sparkling wit and repartee – into someone who was always interested in you and your endeavours. The wife who hardly noticed you arrive home and who never asked you how your day went, becomes, in your imagination, someone who greeted your arrival with delight, eager to listen. The husband who never remembered your birthday, and when he did all you got was a cheap card from the corner shop, is the same man who occupies your imagination now – the one with the huge bunch of flowers and the line in romantic love notes. Selective thinking!

A bit of a reality check does no harm. It helps to talk to your

friends and family and ask them how they saw your marriage.
Ask them to be honest. Maybe, just maybe, it wasn't the perfect
relationship that you remember it to be. Remind yourself that
you've lost some good things, but that you've also got rid of
the bad things too. Remind yourself of some of the things that
your partner used to do that drove you absolutely crazy, and be
thankful that you don't have to put up with them any longer!

Getting stuck

If we're not careful we can get stuck in denial mode, especially if
the parting was sudden and unexpected. In my case, it was very
sudden and very unexpected. It took about eight months before
it finally dawned on me that the marriage was truly over and
that my husband wasn't going to come back; the process took
so long partly because of my husband's refusal to admit that he
wasn't going to return. When I heard that he was in the process
of buying a house with his new partner I finally accepted that
my marriage was dead and buried. Some people can hang on for
years, patiently waiting, putting their life on hold, praying and
hoping, but just suppose the missing partner was to come back?
What kind of a relationship would it be? There is no way we can
return to the past. The relationship that used to be (before the
breakdown) is dead and gone, never to return, and changed
forever. Yes, God can do miracles and I'm sure there are couples
that have been separated for a long time (maybe even living
with other partners) who manage to reunite successfully, but
they are very few and far between. The tension, the lack of trust
and the guilt; all these things will kill a relationship.

Confusion

Others take a long time to pass through the denial phase
because they are bewildered and confused as to why their
relationship came to end. Perhaps there were problems in the
marriage that they were aware of, but they weren't unduly
perturbed about. Perhaps the other partner was much less able
to cope with these problems than you were.

On the other hand, perhaps you were the one who was very unhappy, whereas your spouse was able to cope and didn't recognise that the relationship was in danger. Or maybe there had always been problems, but you managed to keep going anyway and thought you always would, and one day you'd magically become the perfect married couple. Yes, of course you should have communicated these feelings to each other, maybe sought counselling and tried to put things right, but we are all messy, irrational beings who don't always do what the relationship gurus tell us to do.

Unanswered prayer

I don't know why God didn't answer my earnest prayers. Maybe He knew that the relationship would not have survived such an upheaval. Maybe it was His heart to bring us back together, but my husband refused to listen. Sometimes we just have to accept that God is Sovereign; He can do what He wants to do. Maybe He doesn't answer our prayers because He has something better for us. Suppose your partner has left you for someone else and he/she comes back? Could you really go through a repeat performance if it happens again ten or fifteen years down the line? We have to accept that God knows best, that He has our best interests at heart and that if He doesn't answer our prayers, there's a very good reason.

I haven't got any answers. If we had all the answers there would be no need for faith. If we had all the answers God would be reduced to the lowly status of a human being; His thoughts, His actions and His motives open to interpretation and diagnosed according to the gospel of Freud. He would not be the Almighty God, the Creator of the Universe, the One whose thoughts are higher than ours. There comes a point where we have to surrender and stop trying to work it all out.

Turning point

Why are we in denial? It's because, afraid of being alone and terrified of an unknown future, we hanker after the past (the familiar). While you are still hankering and hoping that the relationship will be put back together again, you are in denial. The turning point will come when you are no longer looking backwards over your shoulder at the past, but are looking, no matter how tentatively, into the future.

Denial is not only wishing for the past to be recreated; it can also be denying our feelings, denying that we're hurting, putting a brave face on things and telling the world we're okay too early in the process of separation and divorce. Only by taking a reality check and getting in touch with our true feelings, can we begin to recover.

'There is a time for everything . . . ' (Ecclesiastes 3:1). There will come a day when you can accept reality, when it will not be so frightening. Yes, you will always be scarred and you will carry that scar with you throughout your life. Occasionally the scab will be knocked off and the wound will begin to bleed again; you will be leading a new, different life when maybe you will hear a song that reminds you of the past. Or a memory will pop up from somewhere, knocking you sideways for a moment. It may be a moment, it may be a day or a week . . . but it will be transitory and you will have moved on.

This Too Will Pass Away

If I can endure for this minute
Whatever is happening to me,
No matter how heavy my heart is
Or how dark the moment may be . . .

If I can remain calm and quiet
With all the world crashing around me,
Secure in the knowledge that God loves me
When everyone else seems to doubt me . . .

If I can but keep on believing
What I know in my heart to be true,
That darkness will fade with the morning
And that 'this will pass away too!' . . .

Then nothing in life can defeat me
For as long as this knowledge remains
I can suffer whatever is happening
For I know God will break all the chains
That are binding me tight in 'the darkness'
And try to fill me with fear ...
For there is 'no night without dawning'
And I know that 'my morning' is near.

(Helen Steiner Rice)[5]

Checklist

- Try to avoid looking back at your relationship through rose-tinted spectacles.

- Take a reality check. Remember your partner's bad points as well as the good ones.

- Have as little contact as possible with your partner. You will heal more quickly.

- Understand that no matter how painful it seems, you are making progress.

Chapter 4

Fear

'Have I not commanded you? Be strong and courageous.
Do not be terrified; do not be discouraged,
*for the L*ORD *your God will be with you*
wherever you go.'
(Joshua 1:9)

It is as though the light has gone out and we are suddenly plunged into darkness; we can't see where we're going and there are all kinds of monsters waiting to jump out at us. Mike Riddell puts it this way:

> 'There is a gap between letting go of the old and the arrival of the new. It is the terrible gap of unknowing, the dark space where the unfamiliar is out of reach and the nascent is not quite visible. It is the time between letting go of the rope and discovering whether there are friendly arms to catch you. In such periods we may feel that all is lost and slip into despair. We long for our former securities and mourn their passing. This much is normal and to be expected. Some people become desperately afraid at such junctures. They seek to make their way back to what has gone, or else they become so full of self-pity and regret that they are blinded to the birth of the new when it comes. Times of transition are times of danger, and it is important to learn how to navigate them safely.'[6]

I hardly feel qualified to write this chapter, as I must be the world's greatest worrier. I'm worried if I have nothing to worry about – I must find something to worry about, and quickly! However, I'm working on it, and God is working on it too, but He's got a big job on His hands! As each crisis materialises, and I spend days and nights worrying, He patiently (and with a twinkle in His eye) demonstrates His mastery of the situation and proves to me that I am wasting an awful lot of time and energy that could be better spent on other things.

Try to live one day at a time (I'm also talking to myself here!), as there is little point in worrying about things that may or may not happen. In fact, most of the things we worry about don't happen. What a waste of time and energy! Psalm 37:8 (NKJV) says, *'Do not fret, it only causes harm.'* Worry robs us of our peace of mind and fear is a destroyer of lives and opportunities. Instead of expecting things to turn out badly, try expecting them to turn out well. Life can be a self-fulfilling prophecy – what we expect is what we get. We may not know the details, but God does and He has it all in hand. God's plans will not be thwarted; this is just a temporary 'blip'.

I was afraid of many things: of not being able to cope, of facing an uncertain financial future. I was afraid of growing old alone, of becoming a bag lady, of never being able to find someone with whom to share my life, of never ever having sex again, and of having to go on singles holidays. I was afraid of having to deal with the traumas of everyday life alone. Of decisions that need to be made such as the boiler breaking down, the car refusing to start, or my parents growing old with no one to rely on but me. I was afraid of the huge, empty landscape stretching out in front of me, with all the signposts having disappeared. Where would I go? How would I get there? What would I do when I got there?

During these times, overwhelmed by anxiety, I couldn't pray. I felt paralysed, physically, mentally and spiritually. There was too much to pray about, and too much fear. All I could do was to cry out 'Help!' I had no peace. I would wake up in the morning and my stomach would churn with anxiety.

I remember one occasion when I crashed my car. It was just

after my father-in-law's funeral. I had left after the service to take my son to the railway station in order to catch a train to London. A combination of driving rain, slippery roads, a lack of attention, and emotional distress catapulted my car into the back of the car in front. I returned to the funeral distraught, with a very dented car, and did what came instinctively. I poured it all out to the husband, who had been there for me for thirty-five years; the person who had listened to my problems, comforted me in my distress and made me feel better. The response was nonexistent; he made no comment, except to ask whether our son had caught his train, then returned to my 'replacement' who was sitting nearby. I suppose he found it somewhat uncomfortable to have this highly emotional and distressed woman 'splurge' all over him, especially in front of his new partner. I realised that he was no longer there for me, that he was there for her instead . . . and that when she crashed her car, he'd be there with the sympathy and the practical help. It hurt.

A friend showed me a video recently, of an old man in Burundi who had trekked for miles to reach a refugee camp, having lost his family and his home. He said, 'I didn't realise how much I needed Jesus until I had lost everything.' Unlike him I hadn't lost everything, I had only crashed my car. I guess it's relative, but there comes a point where you realise that you can't always rely on other people. People will inevitably let you down at some stage and ultimately there is only one person who is always there by your side. It's not just anyone, but someone who has infinite power, concern, compassion and love, the Creator of the Universe – a mender of cars (albeit through the local garage) and hurt feelings.

I found it useful to write my fears down. By so doing, I was able to clarify my thoughts and pinpoint specific worries, so that they were no longer a great amorphous fog, paralysing and impenetrable. I could read them out to God and leave them with Him, at least for a few minutes or a few hours until they began to creep back in again.

It's no wonder that people try to run away from fear by seeking shelter in alcohol, drugs, shopping, food, dating or a thousand and one other things – it's anything to prevent the terror from engulfing them.

What the Bible says about fear

The Bible is the greatest self-help book of all. In this day and age, self-help books abound. This is the age of the self-help book, and self-help is a big business to the western world at the dawn of the twenty-first century. When you read these books you come to realise that the wisdom they contain is the wisdom of centuries, the wisdom of many thousand of years, the wisdom contained within the covers of the Bible. It's age-old wisdom and God given.

Over and over the Bible tells us not to fear. Fear in itself is a normal human reaction to a set of circumstances. Jesus experienced fear in the garden of Gethsemene on the night before His arrest. He knew He had to die, and so great was His fear that He sweated blood and asked His Father to take the cup away from Him. But then He said, 'Not my will but yours be done.' He had absolute trust in His Father, despite fear and despite not really understanding what was happening. If Jesus did it, so too can we express our fears and doubts to our heavenly Father, handing it over to Him and trusting Him with the outcome. It is not sinful to experience fear, only to allow fear to paralyse us. Mark Twain said, 'Courage is resistance to fear, not absence of fear.'[7]

Proverbs 3:5 says, *'Trust in the* Lord *... and lean not on your own understanding.'* We don't understand, but we are instructed to trust anyway.

I wrote in my journal:

> 'Father God, I trust you although I don't know what you are doing in my life and my security has been removed. Everything is in turmoil, nothing is certain anymore except that you are God and you have my best interests at heart. You will take care of me because you love me, good will come out of this. I will trust in you Lord, and I will stand.'

We need to speak it out and declare it, even if we don't believe it in our hearts and minds. The spoken word is creative – God created the world through the spoken word. If we speak out positives, and speak out our trust in God every time we feel ourselves being swamped by fear and worry, it will eventually become reality.

To allow ourselves to be paralysed by fear is to demonstrate a lack of trust in God. At times like these, we are being tested on whether what we know in our heads – that God will never ever abandon us or let us down and has our very best interests at heart – has been absorbed into our hearts. If we choose to recognise it, we are being shown the true state of our hearts; what we *really, truly* believe in the very centre of our being. In my journal I wrote, 'Lord, you want me to trust you. You want me to lean on you, to need you more than I need my husband.'

I realised that I couldn't live without God. I could live without my husband, although I didn't want to, but I couldn't live without God.

God is in control

One day it occurred to me (probably with divine enlightenment) that life is like a hand-knitted sweater! The front of the garment is beautiful, the colours skilfully chosen to blend together with superb workmanship, but the back is full of knots where the wool has been joined. When the garment is finished, the loose ends at the back are woven in so as not to be visible. I believe that the knots represent the 'blips' in our lives. The things that have gone wrong, the mistakes that have been made, and the disasters that have happened to us that have caused us to change direction. But the side we see when the garment's worn is without knots, without blemish and a work of art. God can put right any mistakes, join the loose ends together and create something incredibly beautiful.

> 'Some people weave burlap into the fabric of our lives, and some weave gold thread. Both contribute to make the whole picture beautiful and unique.'   (Anon)

A command

The scripture at the start of this chapter commands us not to be terrified or discouraged. It's a *command* because He knows what a destructive emotion fear can be. When we are fearful, and our imagination is working overtime thinking up all kinds of dreadful scenarios that in all probability won't happen, we are not at peace; we cannot be in communication with God and we can't hear His voice. He doesn't say, *'Be still, and know that I am God'* for no reason. We *command* our children not to run into the road and not to stick their fingers in the plug sockets. We don't say, 'If you can possibly help it, please try very hard not to run into the road.' We command them not to do these things because we love them and we don't want them to be hurt. In the same way, God commands us not to worry.

To be fearful is to feel powerless in the face of the evil, whereas what we have at our disposal is something infinitely more powerful – the power of the Holy Spirit.

> *'For God did not give us a spirit of timidity, but a spirit of power, of love and of self-discipline.'*　　　　　　　(2 Timothy 1:7)

Fear throws us into turmoil and panic, where we can't think clearly, causing us to react and to lash out erratically. It's where our molehills become mountains and a single mountain becomes the Pyrenees. Fear blinds us to God and all that He is capable of doing in our lives.

We can safely leave our anxieties in God's hands. Just as human parents look after their children and see to their needs, so too will our Heavenly Father look after us. He knows exactly what we need and He will provide it, whether in terms of finance, housing, or loving and supportive friends – wherever our anxieties lie.

> *'Rejoice in the Lord always. I will say it again: Rejoice! Let your gentleness be evident to all. The Lord is near. Do not be anxious about anything, but in everything, by prayer and petition, with thanksgiving, present your requests to God. And the peace of*

God, which transcends all understanding, will guard your hearts and your minds in Christ Jesus.' (Philippians 4:4–7)

Firstly, we are commanded to rejoice. When God wants to emphasise something, He repeats it and here we are commanded twice to rejoice. It is difficult to rejoice when we are full of worry and anxiety. Worry robs us of our peace of mind. Yet, despite our circumstances, we can rejoice in God, knowing that He has our very best interests at heart and unlike human parents, our heavenly Father is incapable of ever letting us down. Think about the various crises in your life, the times when you were overwhelmed by anxiety and you reached out to God. Did He let you down then? He may not have answered your prayers in exactly the way you had hoped, but answer them He did. You survived, you coped, and you came through.

We are also commanded to give thanks as we pray. No matter what our circumstances may be we all have something to be thankful for. We can be thankful that we can pray with confidence, in the full knowledge that as we 'present our requests to God' our prayers will be answered. We should always praise and thank God *in spite of* our circumstances, not because of them – we shouldn't just choose to thank Him when things are going well in our lives

So, when the worries and the fears creep in remember that the Lord really *is* near, patiently and loyally standing beside us. Loving us, cherishing us, protecting us, intervening in our lives, waiting by the phone. Give Him your anxieties and trust in Him to pull you through – as any human parent would do for a beloved child.

'All shall be well
and all shall be well
and all manner of things shall be well.'
(Julian of Norwich)[8]

Believe it! He is the One who holds the whole Universe in the palm of His hand, who could, with a single sentence, wipe it out forever, as though it had never been. He is quite capable of dealing with you and your problems!

Fear
The true prince of darkness.

Fear for far too long I have cowered at your feet.
Controlled by the insidious lies you used to instil;
    doubt, indecision and shame.

'You'll fail,
It won't work,
You're not good enough,
Something is bound to go wrong.
You're a fake.
No one will take you seriously.
You're way out of your league.'

For far too long your words have stood like sentinels
    blocking the gateway to my redemption.

Fear, you are the true prince of darkness. A monarch to
    the weak of mind and the faint of heart.

You are the greatest robber baron of all time. Day after
    day, year after year a handsome ransom I've paid.
A precious lifetime defined by the constraints of two
    small words ... I'm afraid.

But today my dear prince, your reign ends. Today I will
    take my rightful place as the sovereign of my soul.

I will roar in the face of the beast.
I will throw down a gauntlet and challenge you never to
    step in my way.
I will fight you by night. I will fight you by day.

More than this, my dear prince, I promise for as long as I
    live,
I will lead an insurrection to banish you back to the
    depths of hell.

(Sonny Carroll)[9]

'Peace I leave with you; my peace I give you. I do not give to you as the world gives. Do not let your hearts be troubled and do not be afraid.' (John 14:27)

Checklist

- Tell God about your fears and try writing them down.

- Remember that the Bible is the best self-help book of all.

- Live life one day at a time, trying not to worry about the future or looking back to the past.

- Know that when God says, 'Do not worry,' it's a command. He says it because He knows there's nothing to worry about. He has your future already sorted out. Ask Him to help you navigate this time of transition.

- Look through the Bible. Write down what God says about worry and fear.

Chapter 5

Guilt, Blame and Forgiveness

'For as high as the heavens are above the earth,
so great is his love for those who fear him:
as far as the east is from the west,
so far has he removed our transgressions from us.'
(Psalm 103:11–12)

Guilt is a big one, whether deserved or not. At least it was for me. I was stuck in 'woe is me, what a dreadful wife I must have been for my husband to leave me' mode for months. I was quite happy to accept 100% of the blame and ask if there was any more I could possibly be blamed for. Other people can be totally the opposite, putting the blame squarely on the other partner, bristling with rage and indignation and refusing to accept any responsibility for the breakdown. Neither one is a healthy attitude. A broken marriage is very rarely, if ever, the fault of just one partner.

Regret

There is no such thing as a perfect marriage. All marriages are made up of two fallible human beings who make mistakes, are sometimes tired, sometimes irritable, and who sometimes say and do things that they later regret. Of course there are things you could have done better, times you should have been more caring, more thoughtful. But you didn't, and you weren't.

51

Maybe you were tired or stressed; maybe you were in need of some tender loving care yourself. Whatever the reason you didn't do this or that, acknowledge that you could (possibly) have done it better, vow to try to do it better next time, then ask for forgiveness – from God and from your partner. Then forgive yourself and let it go.

This is easier said than done, as I know from experience. I majored on guilt, wallowed in regret and almost drowned in it, subjecting my friends to a tirade of, 'If only I'd done this, if only I'd done that', 'If only I'd realised he was feeling that way', and 'If only I'd been a better wife.' Then one day a friend pointed out to me, saying, 'Wendy, even if you had done this and that, how do you know he wouldn't have left you anyway?' This stopped me in my tracks and it finally occurred to me that even if I'd done things differently, even if I'd been Mrs Perfect Wife, there was no guarantee that he would have stayed.

Justifications

The partner who has left will attempt to justify their leaving. Maybe they don't really know why they left; perhaps their leaving had much more to do with them and where they were at in their life, at that particular time, than with you. But they have to begin the process of justification, not only so that they can explain to others why they've done what they've done, but in order to be able to explain to themselves. Shortly after my husband left I read the following in a novel:

> 'I know that by now her adulterous brother would have begun the relentless plainsong of the divorce noviciate – pained self-advocacy that hymns the transmutations of love into hatred and indifference.'[10]

I jotted it down in my journal and waited – waited for the justifications to begin arriving. And when they started to come, I took each one and hung it about my person like a huge, heavy unwieldy bag and carried it around. In the end the weight of the combined bags was so heavy that I could hardly walk, I could scarcely function. I had confessed these real and imagined sins before God and had asked for forgiveness, yet didn't feel forgiven, and was willingly taking on board all the guilt, deserved and undeserved.

Conviction v. condemnation

There is a difference between conviction and condemnation. Conviction comes from God, condemnation definitely doesn't. The weight I was carrying around with me (well, some of it) was condemnation; a nifty little pack designed by Satan to rob us of our joy and peace, to enable us to carry the weight of guilt around with us for months, for years, maybe forever. Condemnation is loudly proclaimed from the rooftops for all to hear and is accompanied by a sneer – by disapproval, criticism and pointing fingers.

Our heavenly Father doesn't condemn (there is no condemnation for those who are in Christ Jesus; see Romans 8), He convicts instead. Conviction is a gentle and very private word in our ear from a Father who loves us passionately, who wants us to feel close to Him and wants to bless us. He knows that while we carry guilt around with us, we will run and hide from Him like Adam and Eve in the Garden of Eden. He wants us to shed everything that separates us from Him; all that prevents us from enjoying a close and intimate relationship with Him.

Apologise

It is important that we acknowledge the mistakes we made, and it's a good idea to apologise to the other partner for those mistakes. We can then make a mental note that in future relationships we will endeavour to behave differently and to do things differently. Then we stop looking at the past, turn around and leaving those bags by the wayside, continue on the journey, unburdened by the things that will prevent us living our lives as God intended.

Jeff Lucas tells a story:

'Skegness is s-ooo very bracing!' the holiday poster chortled. Above the caption a rather overweight and jolly cartoon character, dressed in a 1930s bathing suit, danced on the golden sands of Skegness beach, ecstatic with joy that a force-twelve gale was threatening to tear his black-and-white striped swimsuit off.

'Skegness is s-ooo very like an armpit,' I muttered to no one on particular as I strolled along the pebble-dashed beach in the driving rain. Golden sand seemed to be in short supply; crude concrete steps marched down to yellow-foamed stones and rotting piles of stranded seaweed.

Only an hour ago the walk had seemed a wonderful idea. It was raining hard enough to make Noah nervous, and the wind was whipping brown-stained waves into a polluted frenzy. But I was due to speak that night at Spring Harvest 1994. My well-equipped Butlins shed/chalet seemed to be packed with preening female teenagers destined for modelling careers, and little boys who wore rollerblades in the loo, destined for a life in the paramilitary. Hardly a peaceful atmosphere for careful spiritual preparation. Besides, after being at Spring Harvest for eight days I was feeling the need to get away for a while: I was starting to wake up in the middle of the night screaming 'Shine, Jesus, Shine' at the top of my voice ... So I decided to brave the deluge. I felt strangely invincible as I donned my trusty green wax coat – determined, challenged even, to walk the coastline alone.

The security man gave me a pass and a look that said, 'You don't need a coat, pal, you need a strait-jacket,' obviously thinking me mad to venture out on such a day. He was right. The first forty-five minutes presented no difficulties as I walked with the wind at my back, thinking and praying and enjoying the deserted promenade. But the weather was conspiring with the sea, lulling me back into a false sense of security.

When I decided to turn round and head back to camp, my problems began. In a moment, everything changed. The wind was now punching me in the face, a solid smack with each new gust, sharpening the downpour into millions of freezing needles that pricked and numbed my cheeks, I put my head down and stumbled on; but in seconds I was totally soaked, half blind and very, very cold. My jeans clung skin-tight to numb legs. There seemed to be only one solution: to turn around and walk home – backwards. Quickly I looked along the promenade just to make sure that no other escaped lunatics from Butlins were on hand to witness an adult marching backwards along the beach. Feeling very silly indeed, I began the long trek in reverse.

At first if felt fine, a relief even, as the wind battered my back rather than my face. But I only managed a few yards. God hadn't granted me the gift of reverse gear. I was swerving all over the place. It was awkward and uncomfortable. I felt I was going to fall at any moment. After about three minutes, I gave up and turned to face the turbo-charged rain again. It felt like I was lifting my head to the force of an ice-cold power shower, but at least I was heading in the right direction. Despite the weather, to turn around and face the front again was a relief.'[11]

It took me a long time, almost a year, before I came to the conclusion that our marriage had consisted of two imperfect people, that I could have done things better, but then again, so could he; that it didn't have to end the way it did, there were alternatives, and maybe we could have worked things out. But ultimately, what had happened had happened and I couldn't change the past. I could spend years, or the rest of my life, burdened with guilt and regret, with unforgiveness, both against him and myself. It was almost a year before I made the decision to turn around and march into that unknown future, painful and difficult though it was going to be. And some days I would still sit down by the side of the road and curl into a foetal ball. The alternative was to spend the rest of my life (to borrow Jeff's analogy) 'walking backwards'.

Blame

If you are one of those people who puts the blame squarely and totally on the other person – 'they left me, so that makes them guilty, doesn't it?' – then take a long hard look at your relationship and ask friends how they viewed your marriage. Maybe it was not as perfect as you remember when looking back through your rose-tinted spectacles. Yes, there are things that he or she should have done or should not have done, but ask yourself some searching questions.

It can be very painful to acknowledge our part in the break-down of the relationship. We may want to play the part of the victim, the outraged and hard done by, unfairly treated partner, bristling with indignation. It's a sobering experience to come face to face with our own shortcomings but if we are to heal, if we are to go forward into other relationships and not repeat the same mistakes, then it's something we have to do. Having acknowledged your misdeeds and the things you could have done better (your frailties) have grace with yourself. Repent, accept God's forgiveness that is freely and readily given, and then, hopefully a wiser person, move on.

Forgiveness

Let go of blame and let go of bitterness, for as long as you hang onto unforgiveness you are not free. You are still attached to him or her emotionally. You may say, 'But I don't want to forgive them, look what they did to me!' Even if you don't feel you want to forgive them, do it for your own sake. Speak out forgiveness, 'Lord, I forgive . . . ' You will probably have to do it over and over again because forgiveness is a process, not a one-off event.

It has nothing to do with feelings. You will not *feel* that you have forgiven them, but every time you speak out forgiveness it cuts through one of the cords binding you to him or her.

You may not want the cords to be severed, but you have to for your own sake and your own healing. *Forgiveness is for your sake, not theirs.* Forgiveness sets you free from the anguish and the pain, and allows you to move on. It's a decision – a choice not a feeling. We say, 'I choose to forgive.' Matthew 18:21–22 says,

> *'Then Peter came to Jesus and asked, "Lord, how many times shall I forgive my brother when he sins against me? Up to seven times?" Jesus answered, "I tell you, not seven times, but seventy-seven times." '*

We have to do it over and over again until it becomes a reality, and one day we will realise that the feelings *are* there – we have truly forgiven. Remember too, as in the story of the unmerciful servant that is recorded in the same chapter, if we do not forgive others then God cannot forgive us. Not *won't* forgive us, but He simply *can't* as His hands are tied.

Okay, so you may have been treated very badly and yes, it was unfair and of course you deserved better, but prise yourself free from their power to continue to hurt you. We go over and over in our heads what they've done to us. We rerun the video and we subject ourselves to the pain once again every time. It's masochistic; we are allowing them to continue to hurt us, saying to them, 'Come and hurt me again.' Release yourself from that pain and forgive. And maybe forgive yourself for falling in love with someone who has treated you so badly.

> 'It's OK to love someone who is imperfect. God loves all of us equally, he loves you, he loves me, he loves St Francis, his mother the Virgin Mary, the Pope, Adolph Hitler and Judas Iscariot, Jesus loves all these people all equally and each individual, each person named above exactly the same. AND he commands us (you and me) to love one another (including marriage partners) as he loves each of us. Yes, falling in love can be fun, but since the beginnings of time people have been doing it with

unsuitable partners; or have been choosing as marriage partners people who turn out in the long run not to be good for them.'   (Andrew Robinson) [12]

Revenge

Forget revenge. Revenge is a no-no. The desire for revenge (even though it might be fun) churns you up, filling you with hatred, destroying your peace, and preventing you from moving on. If you are plotting revenge you are allowing the other person to continue their hold over you, and you are continuing to allow them to hurt you.

How do you know that you have truly forgiven? Imagine that your partner has asked God for forgiveness for what he or she has done to you. That forgiveness has been granted; the guilt has been lifted from them. They are cleansed and are able to stand before God, head up, accepted, forgiven. How does that make you feel? If you feel cheated, if you want them to carry on feeling guilty, then you have not forgiven! You are like Jonah, who was angry with God because He relented, demonstrated compassion and did not send the promised calamity on the Ninevites.

The best place to be is one where you bless them, wish them well and genuinely want them to be happy, but don't care too much about what they're doing, what they're thinking and who they're with. To be indifferent to them is to have freed yourself from their influence and their power to hurt you, allowing you to move forward unhindered into your future. If you are indifferent they will no longer be able to touch you. Recognise that they are quite probably indifferent to you already; they've moved on, they no longer care what you do, who you're with, what you're thinking. If you still want them to care, then you haven't moved on.

I remember my ex-husband saying to me some time after our marriage ended, that there wasn't a day that went by when he didn't feel guilty for what he had done to our children and me. At that moment I realised that I didn't want him to go through life carrying that huge weight of guilt, that I still loved him enough not to want him to carry that burden for the rest of his life, and that I genuinely wanted him to be happy, for in what way would it prosper me to know that he was unhappy? I think that was the moment I truly forgave. The rest I leave with God.

Look at the scripture at the beginning of this chapter: realise that if you've asked for forgiveness, you have been forgiven. It's as simple as that. God doesn't put your sin into a filing cabinet, to be referred to at some future date. He deletes it. Forgets it. He wipes it out totally and absolutely so that there is no trace left. If you mention it to Him again, He won't have a clue what you're talking about. You are forgiven. That's it. Full stop.

'Forget regret, or life is yours to miss.'

(Jonathon Larson)[13]

Checklist

- Recognise that there is no such thing as a perfect marriage. Accept that we are all imperfect people, that your marriage wasn't perfect and that it didn't have to end the way it did.

- Apologise to God and to your partner for the mistakes you made.

- Forgive.

And don't forget to forgive yourself.

Chapter 6

Loneliness

'The LORD God said, "It is not good for the man to be alone.
I will make a helper suitable for him."'
(Genesis 2:18)

'She was alone that evening – and alone
She had been all that heavenly summer day.
She scarce had seen a face, or heard a tone
And quietly the hours slipped away
Their passage through the silence hardly known
Save when the clock with silver chime did say
The number of the hour, and all in peace
Listened to hear its own vibration cease.'
(Charlotte Bronte, *The Lonely Lady*)

We all experience loneliness from time to time, but the quality of loneliness that comes from being separated from someone we have loved for many years is especially acute. Whether the separation is a result of divorce or bereavement, the loneliness is the same. True loneliness is a physical pain; it hurts in the stomach, it's agonising. I have come to realise that this world is full of lonely people. Lonely people can do mad and crazy things. Lonely people lose all sense of perspective, logic and reason, and can end up in prison or mental hospitals. People need people.

Not only are we alone, but our self-confidence is at an all-time low as well, particularly if we have been left in favour of someone else. We can feel rejected, tossed aside, discarded, unwanted, a failure.

During my marriage I always thought that I'd be able to cope with being alone should the day ever arrive when I would be required to do so. I am an only child, so had been used to my own company whilst growing up. My husband travelled with his job throughout our marriage and, although I missed him, I always quite enjoyed those times, knowing that he would ring in the evening and be home at the end of the week. However, being alone is only enjoyable provided it is a temporary state. When he left for good and I knew he wasn't going to ring that evening to ask me about my day and tell me about his, when I knew he wasn't going to be home at the end of the week, or ever, I discovered for the first time in my life what it is like to feel truly and frighteningly alone.

Aloneness v. loneliness

There is a difference between being alone and being lonely. It's possible to be alone and not feel in the least bit lonely. There again, it's possible to be with a crowd of people and feel lonely. It's possible to feel lonely within a marriage, but having said that, the other person is still there and still occupies a space in your life and provides a level of support, even if communication is not all it could be.

I mostly missed having someone around in the evenings to talk about the day with, to listen how their day went, and to share the details of day-to-day life. I would arrive home and open the door to an empty house, no one there to talk to or to talk to me, no one there to care. Only resounding emptiness and silence.

My husband left in early spring. The summer I'd so looked forward to through the damp, dark days of winter was a nightmare. A summer of long, warm evenings to be shared, spending time together in the garden after work, going for walks and barbecues with friends. That summer, I spent my evenings sitting under the apple trees in my garden. I didn't want to go out, didn't want to run the risk of seeing couples out together enjoying the sunshine. I had to avert my eyes as I passed the pub round the corner from my house, as I didn't want to see the couples enjoying a drink together in the evening sunshine, and I didn't want to be reminded of what I had lost. It seemed as though there were couples everywhere, holding hands and shopping together or sitting in cars together, going somewhere. It was a whole world full of couples.

I was glad when it rained; the dismal weather suited my mood and I remember a surge of relief when I noticed the leaves on the sumach tree turning from green to autumn red-brown, even though it was only the end of August. Bank holidays and weekends were agony. Christmas and Easter can be torture too, as they are times when couples and families get together, when it seems as though everyone has someone. Oh, how easy it is to dive headlong into self-pity at times like these. There is a wonderful little poem by Wendy Cope:

A Christmas Poem

At Christmas little children sing and merry bells jingle,
The cold winter air makes our hands and face tingle
And happy families go to church and cheerily they
    mingle
And the whole business is unbelievably dreadful if you're
    single.[14]

Actually, my first Christmas alone was not the traumatic experience that I had thought it would be. I had a very lovely time with my grown up children who, bless them, organised lots of activities that left little time for being maudlin. And I had a raging cold that included the blessing of a brain that had been replaced by cotton wool and was incapable of thought, rational or otherwise. It might have been very different had I spent that Christmas in my home – the former matrimonial home where many family Christmases had taken place. Instead, I went to my daughter's house in London where there was no 'Christmas past' with which to draw a comparison. Single Christmas number two was even less painful. I do, however, remember Bank Holidays when it seemed as though everyone had somewhere to go and somewhere to go there with, while I was home alone, plunged into doom and gloom, enduring a solitary pity party.

Having survived the first Christmas, the first anniversary, and the first birthday as a single person, you will find it much easier during the second and subsequent years. Accept invitations gladly or invite other single friends round. Make plans, think of something you would really like to do but never seem to have the time, and make it a special 'just me' indulgent sort of day.

Losing your identity

Learning to be alone is a process; you learn to enjoy the freedom that aloneness brings, being released from the responsibilities and demands of others, and being free to chase your own dreams and desires. Especially if, like me, you have emerged from many years of caring for others, of putting other people's needs first, and wearing the badge of wife/husband or breadwinner/homemaker. A huge void suddenly appears in your identity. Those people who do not find an alternative source of identity can lose their way in the dark void that opens up before them, becoming depressed and eventually perhaps, even losing the will to live.

Remember those other identities – mother, father, friend, son, daughter etc. One part of your identity may have been erased but *you* haven't been erased; you still exist and still perform these other functions.

Freedom

However frightening, painful and lonely it might seem, allow yourself a period of mourning, a time of learning to be alone and eventually, appreciating the freedom of being able to do what *you* want to do. At first it won't feel like freedom at all. At first you may spend the empty weekends mourning other weekends (when your marriage partner was with you) thinking of the holidays you enjoyed together, and the anniversaries, Christmastimes and birthdays you spent with each other. But eventually there will come a day when you open the door of your empty home and instead of sensing the ghosts of the past, you close the door behind you and kick your shoes off, breathing a sigh of relief. There may be constraints in the form of children who are still at home, or finances, but there will still be a level of freedom that is at first uncomfortable, then later liberating.

It may be many years since you were last single, and you may have never really discovered who you are – the essential you, before you were swept along on the treadmill of marriage and careers, mortgages and babies. Now is the time to find out not only who you are, but also what you can do and what your real potential is.

Being alone after years of being one half of a couple can be a very scary experience. At first the sense of loneliness and emptiness will be all encompassing, but gradually you will adjust to it. Some of us fill our lives with activity in order to avoid being alone and confronting the painful feelings inside ourselves. We are afraid of silence and solitude because we're afraid of what we might find inside ourselves now that part of our identity has disappeared. This is the part that we need to find and piece together.

Be constructive

Try to spend time alone doing something constructive. Take up a hobby – *do* something. I decorated a room. It was a big room and an ambitious task. It took me weeks, but it was something I could concentrate on and throw myself into.

Take the opportunity to try something new, maybe something you've always wanted to do. Write a poem, paint a picture, find some pen pals on the Internet, learn a language, learn to dance or to play an instrument, take up woodwork . . . anything rather than sit night after night brooding and feeling sorry for yourself.

I have a friend whose first marriage ended some years ago.

She is now happily remarried, but she looks back on that period of living alone as a memorable, happy time: a time when she could be selfish and do exactly as she pleased. It was a time when she could take herself and her bike off for long rides in the countryside at weekends, or be totally self-indulgent in other ways. Maybe, at some point in the future, you too will look back at this time and be able to see much more clearly the advantages of being alone than you can now.

The positive side of solitude

Learn to appreciate the positive side of solitude. Draw up a list of the advantages of being alone, or of being without a marriage partner. At first it may seem that there aren't any, but think – there will be one or two, and the list will grow longer over time. On my original (and pitifully short) list was the freedom to visit family and friends at a moment's notice without having to consider anyone else. Another advantage was being able to watch whatever *I* wanted on TV ... not having to watch the football! Or being able to get up at 3am without worrying that I was disturbing my sleeping husband, and play CDs in the early hours if I felt like it. There is the freedom to make your own decisions without having to take a spouse into consideration, the flexibility to be able to see friends whenever you like, and not having to cook every night if you choose not to. Liz Hurley is quoted as saying that one of the joys of singledom is being able to eat crisps for dinner! I can flop around all weekend in jogging pants and an extremely unflattering T-shirt and it doesn't matter. I can come home at whatever time I like without there being someone looking grumpy because I'm late. Make your own list.

The negative side of solitude

It is easy at times such as this to want to withdraw from the world – and there are times when this is okay, and even necessary in order to reflect. However, long periods alone are not good for us as being isolated can plummet us headlong into self-pity and rejection. Lack of contact with other people causes an imbalance in our way of perceiving the world and our own particular problems. We need others to bring a sense of perspective back into our lives, to give us their opinions on things that we may not be able to see clearly on our own.

Loneliness can be addressed by seeking out the company of others, although there will be times, especially at the beginning, when you feel lonely despite being with people, times when you carry your loneliness with you like a heavy piece of luggage. Being in the company of others, especially at the type of functions that you would previously have attended with your partner, can magnify the sense of being alone. It's alright to say 'no' to some invitations – I couldn't bear to be with couples at first. Seeing couples together and listening to 'couply' conversations only served to remind me of what I had lost. People will understand if you explain, and it will become easier over time. It may be that some friendships will never be the same again – especially those friendships you held as a couple. However, others will replace them.

If your partner has left you, you may have difficulty in allowing yourself to open up and trust others, but the alternative is an existence of isolation, of building brick walls around yourself and of being afraid of involvement in the lives of others for fear of being let down and rejected. We have to realise that in forming relationships of any kind there will always be the potential for being let down, for being rejected. It's inevitable that at some future point in time someone will abuse our trust. However, rather than go through life expecting to be let down and trusting no-one we, as Christians, are instructed to think and expect the best of everyone, remembering that the only one who will never let us down is God. His love remains constant, always.

There are advantages and disadvantages to being alone, as there are advantages and disadvantages to being married. One state is not better than the other, just different, so try to learn to appreciate the positive side of aloneness.

Friends

Friends become all-important at times such as these. Nurture them; speak out your appreciation to those lovely people who care for you. Don't sit in the house waiting for people to contact you, feeling hard done by when they don't ring – ring them.

> 'You can't stay in your corner of the Forest waiting for others to come to you. You have to go to them some-times.'[15]

People are not going to be banging your door down, demand-ing to be your friend. Friendships require work.

Take up new interests and aim to find new friends, friends who only know you as a single person and not as one half of a couple. I was fortunate in that I had a number of single friends during my marriage, friends who became especially important to me when I was single too.

There will be those people who feel awkward; they don't know how to respond to you. I found that some people avoided me altogether, pretending they hadn't seen me. That really hurt, but eventually I realised that it was because they just didn't know what to say. There may also be those insecure people who feel threatened by your newly single state, who can't relate to you in your unmarried state. They will perceive you as a threat to their own marriage, maybe even subcon-sciously suspecting that divorce is infectious!

When Paul wrote his letter to the Philippians, he referred to his friend as a *'yokefellow'* (Philippians 4:3). What a wonderful description of what a friend should be – someone to help carry the load, to share the burden. God never intended for us to do it all on our own; He provides us with people to help share the load. If you are in need of a good friend, ask God for one. He will send just the right person (or people) along.

In your newly acquired single state, pining for a lost marriage and perhaps hoping for a new relationship, it will inevitably be said to you that God is all you need. My answer to this is that

God chooses to demonstrate His love through other human beings; we are all called to be carriers of His love, so there is nothing wrong in desiring love and affection from others – there's nothing wrong in wanting a hug. Single people need to be touched, need to be hugged, and need to be shown affection perhaps more than married people. If a hug isn't forthcoming, ask for one.

> 'We've all been single at some time or another, and none of us are strangers to that terrible all-consuming craving for the touch of a fellow human being. A girlfriend of mine who had been single for four months popped home to see her mother. On the doorstep, her mum gave her a hug, at which point my friend burst into tears, dragged her bemused parent to the sofa, and wouldn't let go for 30 minutes.' (Mariella Frostrup)[16]

I know how she felt! All of us need to be touched. It's a basic requirement of life, almost as essential as food and water.

Churches can sometimes be good places to acquire hugs. Some churches are very 'hug oriented' (sometimes to an alarming degree) whilst others are less so. Remember that during this time of aloneness you may have to ask *for a hug.*

Being still

Try, as far as possible, to view your aloneness as solitude. Use the opportunity to spend quality time with God.

> *'Be still, and know that I am God ... '* (Psalm 46:10)

Being still does not come easy to many of us, addicted as we are to busyness and noise. The Hebrew word for 'still' means 'to relax'. We find it difficult to relax, as we think we're wasting time; we always have to be doing something. It also means 'to sink down', like sinking into the security and comfort of a parent's arms when we were children. It means 'to let go' of burdens, worries and anxieties, to relax into the arms of God; to allow Him to minister to us, hold us, comfort us, and heal us.

To be in the presence of God is to be in a place of healing. We come to God just as we are and allow the darkness and the rubbish to surface without the mask. We come with all our vulnerabilities and faults and it can be scary. So many of us are afraid of our own company, afraid of the voices within, afraid to find out who we really are when the mask is stripped away. We're afraid of being alone and vulnerable. However, standing in the presence of a loving God who knows us intimately and who knows all our faults, allows our sin and our insecurity to be healed, for us to be rebuilt, and to be pointed in the direction of our future.

Nurture your relationship with Him – listen to Him and expect Him to speak to you. Your relationship with God is the most important relationship of all. Friends may move away, marriages may collapse and sink, but God is always there, totally faithful and consistent. Pour out your heart to Him – your anger, your disappointment, your loneliness and your fears for the future. Allow Him to guide, comfort and reassure you. He will always be there for you, both now and for all eternity.

This can be a very special time, when you concentrate on that most important relationship of all. In times to come, times full of busyness and doing, you may look back on this little bit of your life with nostalgia and realise that in the midst of the pain there was a very special time of intimacy between you and God, your very closest friend and loving Father.

> 'Living alone, although it may not be the state you ultimately desire for yourself, affords an unparalleled opportunity to know yourself, to be yourself, and to develop yourself as a unique and interesting individual.'
> (Phyllis Hobe) [17]

> 'It is easier to live through someone else than to become complete yourself.' (Betty Friedman) [18]

Checklist

- Realise that 'alone' is not the same as 'lonely.'

- Learn to appreciate your freedom.

- Try to spend your time alone doing something constructive.

- Make a list of the positive things about living alone. Add to it as time goes on.

- Learn to enjoy your solitude, but don't cut yourself off from the world in the process.

- Cherish your friends.

- Find time to be alone with God.

Chapter 7

Anger

'Get rid of all bitterness, rage and anger, brawling and slander, along with every form of malice.'
(Ephesians 4:31)

Look on the Internet and you will find a plethora of 'cures' for anger. You can buy pills (yes, really!), you can go for hypnosis and/or perform self-hypnosis, and there are videos, seminars and books aplenty by Doctor this or that (I wonder if they really are all doctors?), all offering a magical 'cure'. They all promise peace and everlasting happiness as you learn to deal with your anger. Anger management is big business in the twenty-first century.

Christians have a particular problem with anger, usually focusing on whether they should be feeling angry at all. Problem number two is what to do with it once they've got it. Anger is a very strong, sometimes overpowering emotion; all those uncomfortable feelings surging and seething around, it just feels wrong. But when a marriage comes to an end you have every right to feel angry. Your whole life has been turned upside down. Maybe you've been left, and maybe you've been betrayed. You can feel a sense of betrayal even if your marriage partner hasn't left you for someone else, as you feel betrayed because the future you had planned has been eradicated and your security has been taken away; the promises you made to one another have been broken. Anger is a natural and normal reaction to all of this.

Anger is a physiological and emotional reaction to a set of circumstances. It produces biological changes in the body, as a result of adrenaline being released into the bloodstream. It is an involuntary response – we can't help it. Some people have the propensity to be angrier than others. Some people fly off the handle at the least little thing, taking enormous offence at some casual remark, and being with this kind of person is like living on the edge of a volcano, permanently wondering when the next eruption will come. Others take much longer to erupt. Whatever type of person you are, your 'average response time' will be the result of a combination of genes, upbringing, and how far you've allowed God to change you. We may not be able to stop ourselves from becoming angry, but we have a choice in the way we react and how we choose to respond.

In my own case, because my husband refused to admit for several months that our marriage was well and truly over, I couldn't feel angry with him; to be angry felt like a betrayal, implying that he had done something wrong. I was holding onto hope, and anger wasn't in the picture. However, I felt very, very angry with the 'other woman'. This is a very common reaction – where a husband or wife still has loving feelings towards their partner, and especially where there is still hope, they will project all their anger onto the other party, forgetting that it takes 'two to tango'. If you have been left in favour of another, your partner had a choice to make. He or she wasn't forced into betraying you and leaving you. The 'other person' didn't steal your partner; your husband or wife went willingly. Also, do not allow the 'vanished' partner to heap all the blame and guilt on you, and to insinuate that there was no alternative. There *was* an alternative and what happened was *not* inevitable.

Losing the plot

In my case there were little (oh, okay – not so 'little') flashes of blind rage, in response to circumstances, as things were said and done that I felt were profoundly unfair. I squirm with embarrassment at the memory of some of the things I said, and at these times I became a demented fishwife. Sometimes, the anger was so overpowering I seemed to have no control over it. Although I knew all the right things to do, and knew that I should not be reacting this way, I literally lost control of my feelings – my anger took over. There is a moment when we have a choice; either we exercise self-control, or we let rip and let ourselves get swept away on the strength of the emotion.

Some people hold on to their anger for many years. Full of bitterness, they recount their tale of woe with relish and venom as though it happened yesterday. These people are stuck; they are in danger of going through their whole life locked into 'anger mode', unable to disengage from it, holding onto their hatred – for 'hatred' is what it is – and feeling justified. They tell the story to whoever will listen, regurgitating again and again the pain, the humiliation, the unfairness of it all. Do not become one of these (very boring) people; deal with your anger as best you can with the minimum of damage, then let it go and move on.

Do not allow yourself to be defined by your circumstances, to become a fully paid-up member of the 'Victim's Association'. It's probable that you are getting a lot of attention right now, particularly if you were the one who was abandoned. Like a hypochondriac who thrives on making others feel sorry for them, it's possible to keep on playing the part of a victim long after the drama has ended in order to attract attention and sympathy. I know people who, although their particular crisis happened years and years ago, still wear the victim badge conspicuously on their lapel. Be one who overcomes. Some day in the future, when you are feeling stronger, vow to throw the victim badge away and start living life to the full, as Jesus intended us to. Anger can so easily become bitterness, sinking its tentacles into our hearts and minds and eating away at our peace of mind.

Good anger v. bad anger

Anger is a very powerful motivating force for good or evil. Anyone who feels angry about injustice in our world – about children starving or any other injustice – can be motivated by their anger to make a difference, and to get involved in action that will bring about change. The nineteenth-century reformers who helped to abolish slavery and child labour in factories were motivated by anger. Those who are involved in social action, to get Third World debt written off and to fight for a fair deal for farmers in developing countries whose product will end up on supermarket shelves (only to swell the already overflowing coffers of the supermarket giants), are motivated by anger. The people in Amnesty International, fighting on behalf of the innocent who are held in prison and tortured, are stirred by anger. It is using anger and compassion hand in hand that gets things done, changes the world for the better, and fights for those whose voices cannot be heard.

The other kind of anger – the kind of anger that is without compassion – that wants to hurt, inflict pain, and seek revenge, is the wrong kind of anger. When we refuse to let go, when we become hardened, bitter and full of hatred – this will do us no good at all and will place a wall between God and ourselves. It motivates us to be revengeful, to say hurtful things and to want the other person to pay for what they have done.

So what do we do with this anger? Do we push it down and repress it? To do so would be to create a recipe for disaster. It will re-emerge in some other form – as depression, anxiety, addiction, eating disorders, or psychosomatic illness of some kind. Chronic anger can be costly, both physically and emotionally. There is one way to deal with this anger – not, as I was told in various counselling sessions, to pin my husband's photograph to a cushion and beat it or pin it to the wall and throw darts at it. Forgiveness is the only way.

There is the temptation to say, 'But my anger is justified; this is righteous anger.' That may be true, but that does not give us the right to live with a desire for retribution. Innocent victims can open themselves up to being used by the devil, who loves to stir up hatred; he who *'comes only to steal and kill and destroy'* (John 10:10). If you let him he will rob you of your joy and your health, mentally, physically and spiritually, and may eventually rob you of your life. Not to put too fine a point on it – unresolved bitterness and anger causes stress, destroys our peace of mind, our relationships, and creates illness that can eventually kill us. It will certainly kill our faith and separate us from God.

I believe that God feels angry at the way in which His child has been unfairly treated, just as we human beings get angry when our own children are mistreated. We have to bear in mind too (and this is an uncomfortable thought), that God may be feeling somewhat annoyed with us for being the one who left, or for having made the other person unhappy enough to want to escape from us.

If we seek to inflict pain on the person who has wounded us, if we seek revenge and if we want them to hurt just like we've been hurt, it is quite frankly, a waste of a huge amount of emotional resources and effort that we could be spending on ourselves to build ourselves up. Why waste all that energy on him or her? It's more than they deserve! In your present circumstances, acknowledge the anger and allow it to motivate you to make changes for the better in your life.

What the Bible says about anger

What does the Bible say about anger? It says quite a lot!

> 'In your anger do not sin;
>   when you are on your beds,
>   search your hearts and be silent.'   (Psalm 4:4)

It's back to that moment of choice again. Anger itself is not a sin – it's what we do with it that may or may not be sinful. In our anger we must endeavour not to retaliate – difficult and very tempting though it might be. It's a good idea every night, as your head hits the pillow, to forgive those who have hurt you and ask forgiveness from those whom you may have hurt during the course of the day.

> 'A gentle answer turns away wrath,
>   but a harsh word stirs up anger.'   (Proverbs 15:1)

How to end a slanging match! Do not respond in kind. Things will only escalate. If you succumb to the temptation to lash out, as sure as night follows day, you will lose your dignity and later regret your words and actions. Take a deep breath and put your point over by being quietly and firmly assertive.

> *'Do not let the sun go down while you are still angry.'*
> (Ephesians 4:26)

Keep short accounts. Try wherever possible, to sort things out immediately.

> *'My dear brothers, take note of this: Everyone should be quick to listen, slow to speak and slow to become angry, for man's anger does not bring about the righteous life that God desires.'*
> (James 1:19–20)

At a time like this, when your emotions are raw and messy, it's difficult to respond as you would when things are on an even keel. However, try to keep your anger at bay. I don't believe that God will come down on us like a ton of bricks when we fall short; He is a God of compassion and grace, He loves you and understands. He is *'slow to anger, abounding in love'* (Psalm 103:8). But things said and done in anger can add unnecessary wounds to those who have already been wounded quite enough, and I don't mean him or her ... I mean *you*.

We are ordered to repay hostility with kindness (Matthew 5:43–44), to respond in the 'opposite spirit'. To do so is not easy. It's tempting to lash out, but not doing so will have the effect of immediately disarming your opponent. Sometimes I've managed it. Sometimes I haven't, and responded with all guns blazing.

> *'A fool gives full vent to his anger;*
> *but a wise man keeps himself under control.'*
> (Proverbs 29:11)

God is very patient with me, as He is with you. If you mess up, lose your self-control and find yourself retaliating, don't beat yourself around the head with sticks. Ask God for His forgiveness, accept His grace and be graceful with yourself. Sometimes you get it right, sometimes you don't; you're not perfect – the only perfect person that ever lived was Jesus.

At times the only appropriate response to an unkind word or deed is not to respond at all. It will wind up your ex-partner far more than if you retaliate. You will come out of it smelling of roses and with your dignity and self-respect intact.

Don't allow people to walk all over you; it's possible to stand up for yourself and be quietly assertive without screaming and shouting. Save the screaming and shouting for the privacy of your own home when the neighbours are out, and maybe indulge in a revenge fantasy or two. Keep it a fantasy though. Just think of those writers of the psalms, indulging in the most horrible bloodthirsty fantasies about their adversaries! Then forgive him/her. Speak it out loud, for to do so is to set yourself free. Let it go, for *your* peace of mind.

Anger is a part of the recovery process, so don't feel guilty about it. I was stuck in guilt and denial mode for so long that my friends and counsellors were relieved when I finally became angry. Anger can propel us back into reality, blasting away undeserved guilt – 'I am but a worm' depression and 'he/she was the most wonderful person in the world' denial. Anger is allowed, but just be careful what you do with it.

'If you are patient in one moment of anger, you will escape a hundred days of sorrow.'   (Chinese proverb)

Checklist

- Realise that anger is not a sin; it's a perfectly normal reaction to a particular set of circumstances. It's a healthy response and a necessary part of the process of healing.

- Understand that it's where you allow your anger to take you – what you do with it – that may lead you into sin.

- Do not repress anger. Give vent to it in a safe environment, in the presence of God.

- Do not seek revenge.

- Try to respond in the 'opposite spirit'. Take a deep breath and put your point over firmly and quietly.

- Have grace with yourself when you don't do it right!

Chapter 8

Depression

'Why are you downcast, O my soul?
Why so disturbed within me?
Put your hope in God,
for I will yet praise him,
my Saviour and my God.'
(Psalm 42:5)

In the aftermath of a marriage breakdown many people end up in hospital psychiatric wards or in the doctor's surgery being treated for clinical depression. It is by no means inevitable that everyone will fall prey to depression, but many do and suicide rates are higher for the divorced than for the married or never married.

Symptoms

Some say that feeling sad is an obvious and necessary part of the process of grief and that to take medication in order to alleviate that sadness, is ridiculous. Well, of course it's natural to feel sad, but I'm not talking about sadness, I'm talking about clinical depression – the kind of debilitating illness that can tip people over the edge. The symptoms of depression are insomnia, or conversely, sleeping far too much. In the depths of depression you feel that you don't want to get up in the morning; you can't face the day, and there seems to be nothing to get up for. You become lethargic and lose interest in things that you used to enjoy doing. You are physically and mentally incapable of doing your job or even performing routine daily tasks. You lose your concentration, you don't look forward to anything, you lose your hope, and you cry a lot. Depressed people walk with a stoop and speak in a monotone. Everything seems pointless, and you can become totally overwhelmed by feelings of sadness, remorse and loneliness. Sometimes, you may think about suicide as a way of escaping the constant pain. There is a feeling of emptiness, as though there is a huge gaping hole inside which nothing and no one can fill.

When the doctor gave me medication for depression I felt as though I was a permanent resident on Planet Zog. I was forever bumping into lampposts and staring into space in a vacant sort of way. I felt as though I was drunk! I was relieved of my anti-depressants during a mugging attack while on holiday, and the perpetrators of that particular crime did me a great favour! Hopefully they were bumping into every lamppost in Blantyre, Malawi for weeks afterwards. I had to come off the tablets, cold turkey, but almost immediately, despite the trauma of it all, I began to remember what it was like to feel normal. On my return home, my doctor prescribed another pill for me, one that suited me much better and saw me through the worst of the depression.

Some Christians feel that they've failed if they have to go to the doctor for anti-depressants. They feel that they should have the faith to wait for God to heal them. Yet, if they had a broken leg, they wouldn't think twice about going to hospital for a splint. My own feeling on the matter is that God is a God of variety and He uses many different means to heal us – including doctors and anti-depressants.

Suicidal thoughts

I would occasionally have suicidal thoughts. It seemed like an escape route, when the feelings threatened to drown and overwhelm me. There was one awful, desperate, dark night when I almost did it; I came very, very close to ending it all. I even wrote 'goodbye' notes to my children and my parents, as

I could see no future ahead of me. I lay on the bed wanting desperately to end it all, to die and to escape from the pain. I am ashamed to say that I even put a plastic bag over my head – until it began to stick to my skin and I panicked and tore it off.

I am so grateful to God that He did not let me die that night. People say that suicide is selfish because you are not thinking of the ones who will be left behind to deal with the aftermath, but in truth, at such a point as this, you are not thinking straight or normally, the balance of your mind is disturbed. Looking back, that was my lowest point. If you are feeling like this please, please seek help. Go to your doctor; tell friends how you are feeling. Don't be ashamed of the thoughts in your head. Divorced people are *four* times more likely to commit suicide than married or never married people. Tell God how you are feeling.

My doctor put me in touch with a psychiatric nurse who counselled me for the best part of a year. She was wonderful, putting everything back into perspective, giving me practical advice on how to deal with everyday tasks and problems, and reassuring me that I wasn't going mad!

I repeat – not everyone goes through clinical depression, but many do. What got me through were my children, my friends, my doctor, my psychiatric nurse, my 'Relate' counsellor and last, but my no means least, in the midst of all the pain, glimpses of God's enduring and passionate love for me.

The valley

I remember once, years ago, going for a walk with my family. When we set out the weather was warm and sunny, and the start of the walk was very pleasant indeed. We then found ourselves walking for miles through a long valley, steep hill-sides rising up on either side of us. For miles we trudged through deep shadow, although if we raised our eyes we could see the blue sky and the bright sunshine gloriously lighting up the upper slopes of the hills. I felt rather cheated; it had been so warm when we set out, that I was quite hoping for a suntan! But here we were walking in the cool, deep shadow on goose-pimpled legs, gazing longingly upwards at the sunshine. I remember thinking, 'We'll soon be out of this valley' but no, it went on relentlessly for miles and miles.

I was reminded of that walk recently while reading through Psalm 23,

> *'Even though I walk*
> *through the valley of the shadow of death,*
> *I will fear no evil,*
> *for you are with me;*
> *your rod and your staff,*
> *they comfort me.'* (Psalm 23:4)

Those of us who are mourning the death of a marriage are walking through that valley. It can seem to go on forever, the sadness and the pain of grief. One day, however, you will emerge, out into that glorious sunshine again. Meanwhile, God is there with us, guiding us on to the green pastures. We are walking *through* the valley – we are not staying in it. We're just passing through on our way to somewhere else. And it helps to remember to lift our eyes sometimes, to lift them heavenward, to the blue sunlit skies above . . .

> *'I lift up my eyes to the hills –*
> *where does my help come from?*
> *My help comes from the* Lord,
> *the Maker of heaven and earth.'* (Psalm 121:1–2)

We may occasionally sit down, weary and afraid of going on, but then we become aware of God by our side, urging us to get up, to keep going and giving us hope.

I recently read a magazine article about Nicole Kidman, in which she talked about the end of her marriage to Tom Cruise,

> ' "When it ended, it felt like the end of my life, really. I'm sure many women who go through divorce feel the same. It's a black, black hole." At times she was so paralysed by

sadness that she was incapable of anything but curling foetus-like on the floor. I ask her how she rallied around. She parries with a question, "What makes a child view something as a mountain instead of a molehill? Some children are crushed by adversity, for others it ignites them."'[19]

I'm sure many of us know that 'foetal moment'. I certainly do. I remember an occasion when, one Sunday afternoon and a few weeks after my husband had gone, I wandered into my kitchen to get myself something to eat. Suddenly my mind was cast back to other Sunday afternoons when I would spend hours (I love cooking) making a special evening meal. We would eat and talk together at the table, with wine and candles, then spend the evening together on the settee listening to music or watching TV: special 'together' times. This particular afternoon the kitchen was quiet, empty and unnaturally tidy. There was nothing cooking in the oven, no vegetables waiting to be prepared, no husband. I sank to my knees on the cold kitchen floor tiles, curled up in a ball and wept.

For a while after my husband left I lived in my bedroom. I slept there, crept into the kitchen for a cup of coffee or a plateful of food, and scuttled back with it to the safety of that room. I hardly ever emerged from it; it became my hiding place, the place where I felt safe and secure. I remember lying on the bed during that time and listening to the traffic travelling along the road outside, hearing people occasionally walking past the house. I felt desperately alone, as though the world was going about its business outside my house on the other side of the hedge and here I was, all alone with my grief, and everyone was too busy to care.

I am writing this on a Sunday evening, sitting in front of my computer after a nice chat at the kitchen table this afternoon with a friend, followed, after she left, by a solitary meal. I can honestly say that at this moment I feel very contented, at peace, absorbed and happy to be on my own. Wherever you are on the journey back to recovery, you will experience times of peace and contentment, of being happy in your singleness and as time goes on, these will become the norm and not just the 'now and again'.

Replacing the negative images

You will be very fortunate indeed not to hear yourself spoken of in a negative light at some point after your marriage has ended. It could be your ex-spouse doing the slandering, or their friends and relatives. It's desperately important not to take these things on board. You may be left with negative images of yourself, and these images can have a profound effect on you. Discover what your negative images are and replace them with positive ones.

- You are not *unloved*; you are **loved and cherished.** Your Heavenly Father loves you with a passion. If you feel unloved, you wear it like a cloak. If you don't love yourself then why should you believe that someone else could possibly love you? You will erect barriers around yourself – invisible walls to keep people away. If you are totally convinced that you are unlovable, it is as though you're wearing little badges pinned all over you, all saying the same thing, 'please don't try and love me, I'm not worth it.' Other people will sense something about you and many will back off. You think, 'I am unlovable, don't come near me.' People keep their distance, which reinforces the feeling of being unlovable and off we go again. To put it another way, if you don't value yourself, other people will probably not value you either.

- You are not a *victim*; you are an **overcomer.** A victim is powerless. You are not powerless (if God is for you, who can be against you?) You have the power of Almighty God at your disposal and all you have to do is ask and believe.

- You are not *rejected*; you are **accepted.** As a Christian you belong to the family of God in the same way that you belong to your earthly family because you were born into it. Your name is on God's family tree. You are a son or daughter of the living God.

- You are not *worthless*; you are **treasured**. Your name is carved on the palm of God's hand. You are priceless.

- You are not *abandoned*; you **belong**. God is near you, so near that you could touch Him if you could see Him. He will never abandon you or forsake you.

- You are not *cursed*; you are **blessed**. Because He loves you, God will bless you. He will surround you with His angels and protect you (Psalm 34:7).

- You are not *guilty*; you are **forgiven**. When you asked God to forgive you, He heard and He wiped away all trace of your sin. Refuse to listen to those who might slander you, or heap undeserved blame on you.

- You need not be *ashamed*; you can be **proud** of who you are and what God has created you to be.

    'Those who look to him are radiant;
        their faces are never covered with shame.'

    (Psalm 34:5)

- You are not a *failure*; you are a **success**. There is no such thing as a failure in the Kingdom of God! In God's estimation, you are a success, and He is very, very proud of you.

In the very depths of depression you may not have the resources to pray. But as you begin to feel better, ask God to encourage you and build you up: ask Him to tell you what He thinks about you and ask Him to show you what other people think about you. After my husband left, well-meaning friends and relatives repeated things to me, things my husband had said or that his new partner or her family and friends had said. In retrospect, it would have been far better for me had those people not repeated what they'd heard and it took a long time to wipe out the negative images. I asked God to show me what I really was and what other people – people who really knew me – thought about me. Over a period of time He did just that, using other people to build me up.

Make plans

Try to make plans for the future. Those who can see no future ahead of them are the most likely to go off the rails, to succumb to long-term depression, and maybe seek a 'way out'. It's so, so important to work on your self-image and to make plans for your future, to have something to work towards or something to look forward to and hold onto. The plans you had before – plans for a future with your husband or wife – have been eradicated. But they must be replaced with new plans, and as soon as you begin to feel better you should re-evaluate your life, ask yourself what you would like to do, where you would like to go, and what you would like to achieve – and take positive steps to create the kind of future *you* want for yourself.

Don't forget to include God in the decision-making process because His plans are always far superior to ours.

> '"For I know the plans I have for you," declares the LORD, "plans to prosper you and not to harm you, plans to give you a hope and a future."'   (Jeremiah 29:11)

Count your blessings

In the depths of depression you may not feel that you have many blessings to count, but however dreadful you are feeling, try to remember the old cliché – there is always someone worse off than yourself and there are always blessings to be noticed if we look for them. One day I decided to count mine. Here are some of them, recorded in my journal:

- I have a roof over my head. I'm thinking of all those homeless people right now sitting on cold pavements, or selling the *Big Issue* on freezing January city centre streets.
- I have friends, family and people who care for me. I have two wonderful children.

- I have my health. I am mobile and not confined to a hospital bed or a wheelchair. I have intelligence and mental stability (most of the time!)
- I have a job, an income, clothes to wear and food to eat.
- I am a child of God, my name is engraved on the palm of His hand.
- I'm still alive! Every day that I wake, I know that God still has a purpose for my life.

We can be thankful for the fact that, however dreadful everything might seem right now, God will bring good out of all the mess.

Hebrews 12:28–29 says,

> 'Therefore, since we are receiving a kingdom that cannot be shaken, let us be thankful, and so worship God acceptably with reverence and awe, for our "God is a consuming fire." '

We are receiving a kingdom that cannot be shaken. God will have victory in and through your life if you hold on to Him. We know that He's a God of compassion; He's not just sitting there, patting your shoulder and saying, 'There, there, I really feel for you' and hoping it's going to be okay. He *knows* it's going to be okay. He is Almighty God, a God of infinite and unimaginable power and He's on your side ... if He's for you, who can be against you? So we have everything to thank Him for.

What of the scripture at the beginning of this chapter? The author encourages us to put our hope in God. There is a verse in this same psalm, which is my very favourite verse in the Bible,

> 'Deep calls to deep
>   in the roar of your waterfalls;
> all your waves and breakers
>   have swept over me.'   (Psalm 42:7)

God hears and *understands* the depths of our heart and our being; we don't even need to put it into words. 'Understands' is such a key word as deep calls to deep. Your God knows, He empathises, He cares, and one day we will be shown the purpose of our pain and suffering. Remember that this journey through the valley is temporary and that one day you will emerge into the sunshine and be glad to be alive.

'Happiness is a choice that requires effort at times.'

(Anon)

'Don't be ashamed to need help. Like a soldier storming a wall, you have a mission to accomplish. And if you've been wounded and you need a comrade to pull you up? So what?'   (Marcus Aurelius)[20]

Checklist

- Seek help if you are feeling clinically depressed.

- Don't accept negative images of yourself.

- Count your blessings.

- Know that things *will* get better.

Chapter 9

Disappointment and Hope

'May the God of hope
fill you with all joy and peace as you trust in him,
so that you may overflow with hope
by the power of the Holy Spirit.'
(Romans 15:13)

Disappointment destroys hope and if hope has gone, faith is impossible; we cannot have faith without hope. Essentially we do not believe – we feel that we have been let down in the past and we expect to be let down in the future – we no longer trust God to lead us along the right path.

Disappointment can destroy our peace, our positive self-image and our vision. Disappointment can lead us into isolation, to harden our hearts, to feel resentment of those who seem to have it all together. Disappointment can eventually lead to rebellion and to turning our back on a God, who it seems doesn't care enough about us and has let us down. Being disappointed means not being able to move on; it means being stuck, being preoccupied with the things of the past instead of looking forward to the things of the future. Disappointment is almost inevitable. It's all part of the process of grieving for the marriage, but in order to recover and live life to the full we must at some point – and preferably sooner rather than later – let that disappointment go.

Carrying the rucksack

One day I realised that I was carrying disappointment around with me like a huge, cumbersome, heavy rucksack. The weight of it was dragging me down, and the unwieldy bulk of it was preventing me from getting close to others. I offered up my disappointment to God and asked Him to replace it with a carrier bag full of hope. I left the rucksack at the foot of the cross, picked up the carrier bag and walked forwards with a lighter step. He took my disappointment and gave me back my hope in Him and in the exciting and unknown future that He had in store for me. I thanked God for my twenty-nine years of marriage, for all the good times we had enjoyed together, and for the fruit of that marriage – two wonderful children.

Of course, a few days later I picked up the rucksack again. And had to put it down again. The process of healing, of leaving the past behind, is not a one off event. It's a process of retraining ourselves and allowing ourselves to be retrained.

Victim mode

We can feel like the victim and it's all too easy to get stuck in that role, which is extremely unhealthy. The fact is that we have a choice to make; we can choose to be a victim, to be the hard-done-by injured party and one of life's casualties, or we can choose to say, 'Life is unfair. What has happened has happened. Now how do I get out of this, how do I overcome, how do I start making my way forward?'

I recently had the very unpleasant experience of being alone in the house during the early hours of the morning with an uninvited intruder trying to gain access. Fortunately, he did not gain entry but I was terrified. The policeman who came to take my statement left me a small booklet entitled *Making a Victim Statement*. The booklet sat on the worktop in my kitchen for several days and every time I passed it I thought, 'No! I will *not* be a victim!' At the time I was also struggling with relationship and divorce-related things and that attempted intrusion felt like the final straw – yet another violation. I wrote in my diary,

> 'Right now I feel battered and bruised. I can't get up and fight, can't bounce up and jump about and sing about how wonderful life is. But I can slowly and painfully get up. AGAIN.'

Once, when I was going through a particularly 'sorry for myself' patch my daughter said to me, 'Mum, stop being someone "to whom things happen". Be someone who *makes* things happen, be proactive.' All very well, I thought, but it's not my fault I got stabbed or burgled or abandoned. But I know what she meant. There is something about the 'victim mentality' that can invite disaster and mishap onto our lives. Something we carry around with us, not visible to the naked eye but which shouts to the world, 'Hey look at me, I'm a victim, I'm fair game, come and do something horrible to me.' Stop being someone to whom things happen and be proactive. Good advice.

People can go through life in 'victim mode' because deep down they actually enjoy it. Playing the part of a victim allows them not to have to take responsibility for their life. They can say, 'I'm like this because my parents were horrible to me, because my husband left me, because ...' It's always someone else's fault. Don't allow yourself to be a victim of the past. Lift up your head and, in the words of the song, 'Pick yourself up, dust yourself off and start all over again.'

Trusting again

Some people say, 'I'll never trust anyone again' and this feeling can be very powerful. If we've ventured into a boxing ring and had seven bells beaten out of us, we're unlikely to volunteer to go in there again. As a child, we learn through experience which situations might be unpleasant. We reach out to stroke the cat – the cat bites us; we're very unlikely to approach the cat in the same way again. In adulthood (and in childhood too), someone lets us down, betrays us or abandons us, and we put up the barriers. We say, 'I'll never trust anyone again.' We'll be suspicious of people's motives, frightened of getting close to them and allowing them to get close to us. We're out in the cold and the end result is that we may live forever within the confines of those brick walls. However, an essential part of close human relationships is the ability to trust, to open up, and to be vulnerable (within the confines of common sense).

God wants to send others across our path, people who will love us, cherish us and nurture us. People whom God wants us to love and cherish in return, and in order to experience and give that love, we need to let go of disappointment and rejection and the inability to trust. To do otherwise is to close the door on life and all it has to offer us.

Hope

There were many times when I all but lost hope. I recorded this in my journal,

> 'It is during times of crisis that we discover what we really believe. We've read the words, we think we understand them, we think we can trust God to give us the best. But deep down, I at any rate, don't believe that God will give me the desire of my heart. Deep down I believe he's forgotten me, I'm the name he's forgotten to put on the list.
>
> *"He who dwells in the shelter of the Most High*
> *will rest in the shadow of the Almighty.*
> *I will say of the Lord, 'He is my refuge and my fortress,*
> *my God in whom I trust.'"* (Psalm 91:1–2)
>
> Do I really trust him? I can speak the words but deep down, at this moment, do I really believe it? Maybe not. Or maybe I did once but now everything seems to have gone pear-shaped and I have drifted away, drifted away from the shelter. When I pray, do I really believe he can hear me?'

I am so grateful that we have a God who understands our doubts and knows us inside out. He doesn't say to Himself, 'Oh she's a waste of time, how many times have I told her she can trust Me and here we are again. I think I'll leave her to stew in her own juices.' No, God keeps carrying on, patiently demonstrating His love, proving to us all over again that He can be trusted and that we can expectantly and safely place our hope in Him.

Reading through my journals has been an interesting experience. So many times, over and over, I would write about how God had encouraged me – about how a piece of scripture had spoken to me and about how positive I felt; about how I had seen the light and had surrendered it all to Him and about how I was placing my trust and my hope in Him. And yet the following day or the following week there would be an entry along the lines of, 'Woe is me, all is darkness, I can see no chink of light, no hope.' This happened so many times that it's funny.

God is so patient with us, so steadfast, so loyal, through all our doubts, all our doing it our own way and leaving Him out of the picture, and through all of our despair and unbelief. He keeps walking with us, demonstrating His love for us. It's a slow process, but God is not in a hurry; He will give it as much time as it needs, until we finally learn the lesson – that no matter what garbage life throws at us there is always hope: hope in a God who wants to do things His way because ultimately, He knows what is best for us and has our very, very best interests at heart.

The greatest self-help book of all – on the subject of hope

The Bible says a great deal about hope:

> *'I rise before dawn and cry for help;*
> *I have put my hope in your word.'* (Psalm 119:147)

Read the Word of God, read the promises He has made to you. Read how He will never abandon you, never forsake you, and how He has a plan for your life: a plan to prosper you and not harm you, a plan to give you a hope and a future (Jeremiah 29:11). Read about how much He loves you and cares for you, how He cherishes you, how you are engraved on the palm of His hand, and how He rejoices over you with singing. There are hundreds, thousands, of promises and declarations of His love for you, written right there in His Word. Do you think they apply to everyone else in the Universe but not you? Do you think He's a liar? These promises are given to you personally. Be assured that God will never, ever let you down and that you can put your hope in Him; not in relationships, not in things, not in having money in the bank or insurance policies, not in finding another marriage partner, not in career success or worldly possessions or aspirations, but in God, the One who is in control of the Universe and everything in it.

> *'... And we rejoice in the hope of the glory of God. Not only so, but we also rejoice in our sufferings, because we know that suffering produces perseverance; perseverance, character; and character, hope. And hope does not disappoint us, because God has poured out his love into our hearts by the Holy Spirit, whom he has given us.'*   (Romans 5:2–5)

Through our suffering we will obtain perseverance and character, and through these things, hope. How else can we learn to lean on God and God alone, than through having our crutches removed?

All the plans I had for my future, a predictable future with my husband (I was to learn that there is no such thing as a predictable future), were whisked away in the course of a single day. But how exciting to have my plans replaced by a whole new set of plans – God's plans. He's much more imaginative than I am and I wait in anticipation to see what He's got up His sleeve for my future.

We don't learn about the character of God when everything in our life is going smoothly. Instead, we learn the reality of God's love for us, the reality of the promises He has made to us, when everything goes wrong, and when we can no longer rely on our own understanding; In times when *'the fig tree does not bud and there are no grapes on the vines'* (Habakkuk 3:17).

The scripture at the beginning of this chapter – *'joy and peace'* – goes hand in hand with trust: to trust in an all-powerful God and Father who is besotted with us. Our inheritance is not disappointment and bitterness, unless we choose these things. As children of God, hope, joy and peace are our inheritance.

> *'Even youths grow tired and weary,*
> *and young men stumble and fall;*
> *but those who hope in the* LORD
> *will renew their strength.*
> *They will soar on wings like eagles;*
> *they will run and not grow weary,*
> *they will walk and not be faint.'*   (Isaiah 40:30–31)

'Blessed is the man who expects nothing, for he shall never be disappointed.'   (Alexander Pope)[21]

'Hope is the dream of a soul awake.'   (French proverb)

'Experience is not what happens to you; it's what you do with what happens to you.'   (Aldous Huxley)[22]

Checklist

- Let go of disappointment; it will affect your relationship with God and with others. Make an exchange – your disappointment for God's hope.

- Allow yourself to be vulnerable and to trust again. Avoid building the brick walls – or do some demolition work!

Chapter 10

Recovery:
Rebuilding Your Self-Esteem

'... and love your neighbour as yourself.'
(Matthew 19:19)

When a marriage ends, particularly if it didn't end by mutual agreement and you were the one who was left behind, your ego and sense of self-worth can be all but annihilated. You will feel that you were dumped, you weren't wanted, and that you were rejected by this person who probably knew you better than anyone. It is as though your essential self – all that you are – has been rejected and cast aside.

Love yourself

It's all too easy to go marching down the 'I'm a worthless nobody, I am but a worm' road, and you'll need to do some work on building up your self-esteem by being a bit selfish for a while. As Christians, we feel that being selfish is not quite the thing to do; that we should be 'dying to self', and always giving to others. But what about the scripture at the beginning of this chapter: *'love your neighbour as **yourself**'*? You need to love yourself first before you can love others, and you're probably not feeling very positive about yourself right now. You won't be able to get back into neighbour-loving mode until you've deleted at least some of those negative images of yourself that your particular trauma has bestowed upon you. At this point in time, God is carrying you and you are in no fit state to carry others, although that time will come – you can be sure of that. The time will come when you will have the opportunity to reach out to others who are going through the same pain that you're enduring now, but for the time being it's right to look after yourself and to learn to like yourself first.

Making changes

I would wake in the morning and turn over, expecting, in my half-comatose state, to find my husband lying beside me as he had done for twenty-nine years. However, I would discover an empty bed instead. Eventually, though it took me some time, I realised that I did not need to continue sleeping in that double bed or even in the bedroom we'd shared together for years. I moved myself into another bedroom and into a single bed. The joint bedroom became a guestroom and I no longer had to wake in the morning with reminders all around me. It's quite a small thing, but in those early days it was a big step for me in the process of learning to survive alone.

It took me a very long time to realise that I didn't have to sleep on one side of the double bed. Some two-and-a-half years after he had left I experienced a very rude (and painful) awakening when, during a particularly vivid nightmare, I ducked sideways to avoid something swinging towards me … and fell out of bed! It then occurred to me that I didn't have to sleep on the edge, because there was no-one occupying the other side, and that I could spread out in the middle! (Talking about beds, I disposed of the marital bed we'd shared for years and purchased a pristine, never slept-upon, new bed – just for me!)

Make some changes in your life. This is a new life; maybe one you wouldn't have asked for, but a different life, and it's largely up to you how it develops. Even very small changes, like ordering a Sunday newspaper when you didn't have one before, having your hair cut short when you've had it long for years, or joining an evening class, give you back the control of your life, building up your confidence little by little.

Other people's expectations

Ignore other people's expectations. They may expect you to carry on doing this or that. They may think it will do you good to get involved in something to take your mind off *It*, but your energy levels will be very low – you need all your energy to cope with your emotions and the stress of separation and divorce. So, don't worry about what other people think; it's now time to practise saying that very difficult word – *No* – especially if you've always been someone who always says, 'Yes.' If people have difficulty with you saying no, that's their problem, not yours. They will probably not have been through the experience that you're going through now, and they simply can't understand.

Trumpet-blowing time

There are a number of practical steps that you can take to work on your self-esteem. For the time being, I suggest you shelve your responsibilities and spend time on yourself, because just now you are Number One. You've been through this traumatic experience and you need a time of recuperation, to build yourself back up again.

Make a list of your gifts and your positive attributes. Ask your friends for their input – how they see you, what do they consider to be your good qualities. Write or type a list out and pin it somewhere where you'll see it on a regular daily basis. Keep a copy in your purse, wallet, bag and car, and when the negative thoughts start to come, as they will, read through it and read it aloud. Your list could say, 'I make people laugh, I'm kind, I'm generous, or I'm a good mother/father.' This is trumpet-blowing time; forget all that modesty stuff.

Dreams and ambitions

During a marriage we can live such routine, blinkered lives. In the midst of the busyness we say to ourselves, 'One day I'll do this ... or that,' but that day never comes. Look upon your newfound freedom as the opportunity to turn those dreams into reality.

Make another list and write down all the things you've ever wanted to do. Maybe some of them will be childhood dreams that you've dropped somewhere along the way. This is your 'Desires of the Heart' list. Nowhere on it should it say, 'I want another husband/wife'. This is about you, not you plus someone else.

My daughter suggested that I should do this shortly after my husband left but there were pitifully few things on it at first. Years of looking after a family and putting their needs first had erased my own ambitions and dreams. On that list, I wrote:

> 'Learn flamenco.'
> 'Live by the sea.'
> 'Get fit.'
> 'Write a book.'

I booked flamenco lessons that autumn and had a wonderful time (although I wasn't very good at it) stamping and swirling my skirts, looking snooty and doing twirly things with my arms and hands. The flamenco lessons came to a somewhat abrupt halt when I went on holiday to Africa with my daughter – only a few weeks into the term – and managed to get myself attacked and stabbed in the hand. Three months in a rather fetching bright green plaster cast put paid to the flamenco and the hand twirling for a while, but it had done me no end of good.

I spent many happy hours on the Internet looking for nice little houses by the sea – until I realised it was a rather silly idea. Yes, I could now choose to live anywhere I wanted, but I'd be leaving my friends and family behind, wouldn't know anyone, and realised that I'd probably hurl myself into the briny within three weeks. But I had a nice time daydreaming. I may yet move to the seaside, but for the time being I will stay near to my friends and family and the people who love me, despite the danger of bumping into my husband and his new partner in the supermarket.

I joined a posh gym, taking advantage of the special daytime rates; pumping iron is a wonderful way to release pent up adrenaline. After a hot shower (making full use of the gym's lotions and potions) I felt great. It was very satisfying to see all those calories being clocked up on the treadmill, the bike or the rowing machine. A brisk walk in the fresh air is every bit as good (if not better) than an hour in the gym and you will feel loads better when you come back.

And the book? I'm in the process of writing it now.

Maybe you've always wanted to learn car maintenance or Chinese, or learn to sing or paint ... whatever it is, go for it! Is there a place you'd really like to visit? Skegness or Bangladesh? Then do it! If you can't afford it right now, plan to do it within the next few months, or years. Send for the brochures and start to plan.

It is good to get away from your day-to-day environment and go on a trip somewhere. Take a holiday, or spend a few days with friends or family. The very experience of being in a different place physically, allows us to 'think outside the box' – to explore all kinds of possibilities that elude us while in the familiar and possibly stifling environment of home. Somehow, things that may seem impossible or too scary to contemplate while in the confines of our own environment take on a different perspective when we go away. We think, 'Well, what's to stop me from moving to a Greek Island?' (I went through a Greek Island stage!) or 'Why shouldn't I set up a teashop/ask for promotion/be the managing director of a multi-million pound business empire?' Give your imagination free reign. Okay, so some of the things on the list may be a few steps too far in the direction of impossible (or maybe not, because with God nothing is impossible), but it's exciting to think that you really can change your life and do things you might never have done.

My turning point

This brings me back to Africa and the stabbing incident. I was on holiday in Malawi with my daughter when a gang of local muggers decided to relieve me of my hand luggage. In order to do so, one of them stabbed me in the hand. On my return to the UK I had to undergo surgery to repair the severed tendons and spent three months in a plaster cast. I had to wait for friends to come round to the house before I could have a shower, as I needed them to tie a plastic bag around the cast to stop it getting wet! I couldn't drive, so was forced to ask for lifts, couldn't cook, so lived on microwave meals for many weeks, and couldn't mow the lawn so had to ask friends to do it. All this, despite being a pain, was very good for my 'independent streak', my pride and my stubbornness!

Friends tell me that when I returned from that holiday I changed; it had been my turning point. I got angry, not so much with my husband, but with the devil. I thought, 'How dare you!' That was the point when everything turned around, where I picked myself up. One Sunday morning I declared in front of a packed church that the devil could rob me of my husband, my home, my security and my future but he wasn't going to rob me of my God. I got angry! As the applause erupted, taking me totally by surprise, I thought, 'Goodness me, did I really say that?' But I would like to think that on that Sunday morning there was applause in heaven too, and that God was smiling, probably grinning from ear to ear.

Finding out about you

Find out who you are, and what your likes and dislikes are. You will discover that you can watch whatever you want on TV, and that it may not be the same type of programmes you watched with your marriage partner. You can take out a video or go to the cinema to see a film that you wouldn't have dreamed of going to see with him/her. You can eat whatever you want to eat and wear whatever clothes you like.

My husband didn't like me in high-heeled shoes. It took me a while, but one day I went out and bought myself a pair of sandals with high spindly heels. They were very uncomfortable, totally impractical and I could hardly walk in them, but it felt wonderful to wear those shoes! He liked me with short hair but I'd always liked my hair long, so I grew it. After a few weeks I realised that I could move the furniture around, move pictures or take them down altogether, paint my bedroom ... or any other room for that matter, any colour that *I* wanted.

When I met my husband at the age of seventeen, I was a very shy and insecure individual who didn't have the faintest idea who she really was. When my husband left thirty-five years later, he took with him a part of my identity and also our CD collection. What was left of the collection made a pitifully small and motley pile and I realised that I didn't actually know what kind of music I liked. My husband had been the one who had bought the records, the cassette tapes and, later, the CDs. I just listened to his taste in music, some of which I liked and some of which I didn't. There was an element of me thinking, during all those years of raising a family, that I shouldn't be spending money on such frivolities – a peculiarly feminine trait! After my husband left, I went out and bought myself a CD player that I couldn't afford, and set about finding out what kind of music I liked. My children, both in their twenties, played their CDs to me, and the ones I liked, I bought. Next, I went out and replaced the ones my husband had taken, the ones I'd really liked. Later still, I spotted a shelf of 'Golden Oldies' by the cheese counter in the supermarket and added one or two to my trolley. I was like a kid in a candy store; I had a wonderful time filling in the gaps. I called it 'recreating my past'. At first I bought only new releases and classical music. Every piece of music from the last third of the twentieth century reminded me of him, and for a year I couldn't listen to any of that music – it was far too painful. My breakthrough came when I bought a CD of songs from our 'courting' days and was able to listen to them without dissolving into floods of tears.

Comparing yourself with others

We are each unique, all different; your way of coping with things may be different from mine. I have a friend who, after her husband of twenty years left her, locked herself in the house, played all the music that reminded her of their time together and cried non-stop for two weeks. She says it helped her to get over him quicker – she got all the crying over and done with in one go! She looked at photo albums of their time together and cried some more. I couldn't do that. I hid the photo albums away on the very top shelf of the wardrobe so I wouldn't see them every time I looked in there. I removed all the photos of my husband shortly after he left – our wedding photo, the one of us looking happy together on a bench in a field of bluebells, photos of the whole family, holiday photos; I couldn't cope with coming face to face with him every time I entered my dining room.

Sometimes, I felt that my friend was handling things far better than I was. What I forgot was that we are all different and we were both dealing with the process in our own way. My way was not inferior to her way – just different. Try not to compare yourself unfavourably with others.

Pamper yourself

This may seem very 'unspiritual' – but never mind! Do whatever you can to feel good about yourself. I lost some weight; a very welcome by-product of extreme misery and lots of adrenaline rushing round in my bloodstream for months on end. I had to buy new clothes that were two sizes smaller. Friends said that I looked wonderful . . . and younger.

Try not to overdo the dieting though. Human beings seem to have a built-in mechanism to deal with pain. Sometimes, in an attempt to block it all out and not think about *It*, we overeat or drink too much, or start to behave like teenagers, dating whoever we can lay our hands on; or we go overboard on exercise and dieting. When we start to lose weight and friends say how good we look, there is a danger of succumbing to eating disorders. It's as though everything is out of control and this is one area of our life that we have the ability to manage. There may be something in you that thinks, 'I'll show him . . . or her. When they see me, they'll be sorry they left.'

Eat properly; this is so important right now because you need to be physically and mentally strong. As well as all this emotional stuff, you will be trying to cope with practical matters too – solicitors, divorce, dealing with all the financial implications and maybe moving home. So please look after yourself.

For the first few weeks after my husband left, I didn't cook a meal for myself – I just couldn't be bothered. I didn't think it was worth cooking just for me and would go all day without eating, realising at 11pm that I was ravenously hungry and devour whatever was in the fridge or the cupboard. There is a tendency for newly single people to eat straight out of the packet. It was too much trouble to get a plate; I would cook frozen ready-made meals in the microwave and then consume them out of the container they came in. Try to sit down with a knife and fork, just as you would have done had someone been sharing it with you.

I booked a course of ten sun bed sessions. Not for everyone maybe, but it made me feel good about myself to have a tan just as the weather turned warmer and people were shedding the winter layers.

Money might be tight, but buy yourself that face cream, that shower gel, or have that hairdo. I'm not encouraging you to spend wildly (I hope), but treat yourself; it's all part of the process of deleting the negative image you might have of yourself and replacing it with a new, confident, 'I value myself' persona.

Just look after yourself. If you had a friend who was going through what you are going through now, you would make sure she was looked after, so do the same for yourself. Not to look after yourself is to say, 'I'm not worth it.' Yes, you are!

Days off

Have some 'doing what I want to do' days. If that means you can't go to that church meeting, or visit your aged uncle, then so be it – they'll survive without you. Stop worrying about what other people might think; if they're upset or annoyed with

you, that's their problem, not yours. You are not responsible
for their feelings.

Set aside a whole day on a regular basis to do what *you* want
to do. Take a trip to the seaside, take the children or someone
else's children, go on your own, or with a friend. 'On your own'
is okay; 'on your own' has its advantages. You can walk along
the beach and kick pebbles and you can do the things you
would like to do without having to be concerned that someone
else might really want to be doing something else.

Or you could spend all day in bed if you want to, pretending
you're not in. Ignore the phone and the doorbell and be
self-indulgent. Watch soppy videos and eat chocolate all day
if you want to – yes, I know I just said all that stuff about
eating properly and so you should – but once in a while it
won't hurt. Spend all day reading novels, spend the day with a
friend, spend it doing something that will make you feel
better.

Choose your friends

Talking of friends, if there is anyone who does not encourage
you or is not understanding about your roller-coaster emotions, who criticises you and who says, 'You should be over this
by now', or who makes you feel guilty, then avoid them like
the plague. Right now you need them like you need a dose
of the flu. Surround yourself with positive, affirming, loving
and encouraging friends and family.

Choose to believe what these friends – and all the people
who love you (including God) – think about you. It is part of
the human condition that if someone says lots of good things
about you and one negative thing, we'll home in on the
negative thing because deep down, that's how we feel about
ourselves. Let it go, forgive them, and choose to only listen to
those people who have your best interests at heart and who
wouldn't dream of being negative about you.

True friends will understand that there will be times when
you seek out their company and other times when you want
everyone to go away, when you need time on your own. Real

friends will understand that you need space at times, and they will not be offended.

Laughter

Some days I felt as though my face would never smile again, as though it was permanently fixed in misery. Laughter is a great healer, a brilliant way of putting things back into perspective; sometimes it really is 'the best medicine'. It has been shown that laughter reduces levels of the stress hormone epinephrine, as well as boosting the immune system, and this is possibly one reason why depressed people who don't laugh much fall prey to illness more easily. Laughter provides a safety valve, a way of releasing pent-up emotion.

Spend time with friends who make you laugh, take out a funny video, watch a comedy programme on TV, read a funny book and laugh the negative emotions away. Remind yourself that you have every reason to laugh – you can 'laugh at the days to come' in the knowledge that your future is in your Father's capable hands.

Spend a day with God

Spend a day with God – light a candle, talk to Him, ask Him to talk to you, and listen. Don't forget to have a notebook and pencil at the ready to write down what He says. Ask Him to tell you His opinion of you and ask Him to show you how much He loves you. Read your Bible and copy out all those passages where God tells you what *He* thinks of you. When He tells you that He will never leave you or forsake you He's talking personally to you, not everyone else!

Remember that God is in control and that He will always bring good out of bad situations. One day, your life will be totally different; you will feel joy and peace and contentment again. You will meet people and do things that you couldn't even begin to imagine now. He will rebuild and restore you. The future that God has in store for you is exciting. Step into it with a thankful heart.

'The most wasted of days is the day when one did not laugh.'   (Nicholas Chamfort)[23]

(Well, It made me laugh!)

'There are no impossible dreams; there is just our limited perception of what is possible.'   (Anon)

'The opportunity that God sends does not wake up him who is asleep.'   (Senegalese proverb)

'. . . *Do not grieve, for the joy of the* LORD *is your strength.*'
                    (Nehemiah 8:10)

Checklist

- Be selfish – do what *you* want to do for a while.

- Do not be influenced by other people's expectations of you.

- Make a list of your good points; your talents.

- Seek out the company of people who encourage you.

- Don't compare yourself with others.

- Make another list of your hopes and dreams. Think about how you could make some of them a reality.

- Occasionally move yourself out of your home environment, and allow yourself to think outside the box and dream.

Chapter 11

Beauty in Unexpected Places: Living in the Moment

'My heart is not proud, O Lord,
my eyes are not haughty;
I do not concern myself with great matters
or things too wonderful for me.
But I have stilled and quieted my soul;
like a weaned child with its mother,
like a weaned child is my soul within me.'
(Psalm 131:1–2)

At times like this, after a painful separation and seeming to be at the mercy of our emotions, we can appear to spend all our time either living in the past or in the future, and in so doing we miss much of what is happening in the here and now. We spend our lives bogged down in the past, regretting past mistakes, reliving traumas, and yearning for bygone times when we were happy. We are caught like a fly in a web of memories, unable to struggle free into what is waiting for us in the here and now. Or we may spend time imagining an unknown future, a future full of uncertainties and difficulties, of anxiety and fear.

Now and then, we find ourselves conscious of the moment; we hear the birdsong, are captivated by the beauty of a dark blue-grey sky just before the rain starts to fall, are aware of the heat of the sun on our backs, or captivated by the smile of a child. We hear the church bells or look into the night sky and

111

notice infinity stretching out above our heads. As I look back on my journey through the valley, I remember several of these moments, times when I became briefly aware of the world around me, when I experienced a sense of joy and peace – a sense of God being in control in the midst of all my pain. Those memories serve as landmarks to me, signposts from God saying, 'Hey, lift up your head and stop staring at the pavement, look at this. Don't worry, I am in control.'

From time to time, in the midst of the grieving, I would catch a glimpse of the 'now' (the moment) and with this moment, sense the presence of God – a sense of eternity and a sense of awe at the incredible beauty of the Universe and of its Creator; such as a huge, yellow moon suspended in the sky at 2am one sleepless night, seen between the gap in the bedroom curtains. Or another moon, this time the biggest full moon I've ever seen, hanging low like a vast, orange balloon in the blackness of an African sky. Or sunlight sparking on water, drops of rain after a shower, clinging like tiny diamonds to the leaves of a plant in the garden. A sense of God being totally in control and of Him wanting me to step aside for a moment, out of my pain and out of the worry, the fear and the anger, to show me something beautiful – to take me by the hand and enable me to catch a glimpse of eternity. The poet R.S. Thomas understands this,

The Bright Field

I have seen the sun break through
to illuminate a small field
for a while and gone my way
and forgotten it. But that was the pearl
of great price, the one field that had
the treasure in it. I realise now
that I must give all that I have
to possess it. Life is not hurrying
on to a receding future, nor hankering after
an imagined past. It is the turning
aside like Moses to the miracle

of the lit bush, to a brightness
that seemed as transitory as your youth
once, but is the eternity that awaits you.[24]

When you find yourself thinking about the past, remembering the hurt and pain, concentrate instead on the present
moment. Just stop, close your eyes, and become aware of the
sounds around you, of what is happening *now* around you.
From time to time, step out of the past and the future, and
become aware of the present moment. It is inevitable that you
will spend much time mulling over the past, and inevitable too
that much of your energy will be expended on thinking about
your future. You spend a huge amount of time dealing with the
practicalities of divorce, filling in forms, meeting with your
lawyer, maybe job hunting or house hunting. You may be
carrying the whole burden of looking after the children and
ferrying them to their various activities when, before the
breakdown, the burden was shared.

A month before my husband went I was due to drive down to
the south coast to attend a four-day conference. It was my
birthday and I asked God for my customary present from
Him – not a rainbow this year, but tulips. The day went past.
I received various presents but no tulips, real or otherwise. I
set off to drive the one hundred and eighty miles to the
conference. Along the motorway, I stopped for a break at
the services and, walking into the ladies toilet, I saw a vase
suspended halfway up the wall holding a bunch of tulips! The
words came to me, 'beauty in unexpected places'. A bunch of
tulips halfway up a toilet wall: Beauty in unexpected places. It
was a phrase that would come back to me over and over in the
months that followed, during my particular storm.

The year before my husband left (I wonder; will time be
forever delineated according to pre-when-my-husband left and
post-when-my-husband-left? I hope not!), a friend and I went
to the Lake District for a few days. We decided not to plan
where we were going, but just to get in the car and go. We
asked God to plan our journey and take us to wherever He
would have us go. We had a wonderful few days. At times we

could almost hear His voice saying, 'Now go around this corner, go along this road, now turn left.'

One day during this trip I wrote in my journal:

> 'This morning Annie and I went for a walk through some woodland. A decaying log caught my attention and I stopped for a moment to look closely at it. There were so many different kinds of moss and lichen growing on this log, all colours, all shapes, a mini-forest. Different colours, different shapes, like tiny, minuscule trees. Quite extra-ordinarily, enchantingly, mesmerisingly beautiful. All this happening on a rotting piece of wood that normally I'd just have walked past and not registered.'

Later we visited John Ruskin's house at Brantwood, and as we walked into his study, I noticed a glass dome on the desk. Under the dome was a piece of log, covered in every kind of moss and lichen and he'd written about it, describing in detail the shape, the colour, and the form.

The whole point of the exercise, I decided on that occasion, was for God to say to me, 'Stop, Look and Listen.' Even on a rotting piece of wood there is beauty, and even in the midst of incredible pain and sadness there is beauty – if we open our eyes to it. The beauty of a rainbow, the night sky, a sunset, or a field illuminated for a moment by the sun. The beauty of family and friends exhibited through their love, their caring, and their support. One day (if you haven't already done so), post-trauma, you will wake in the morning and instead of remembering – instead of the fearful thoughts flooding in – there will be a sense of peace and well-being, a sense of being glad to be alive on this day in history.

Sometimes, in order to be able to 'stop, look and listen', it is necessary to create a space in the turmoil of our busy lives: A time to sit or to lie, to maybe light a candle, to be 'still' with God. To allow Him to say, in a million creative ways, 'Don't be frightened, trust Me.' For Him to say, 'I love you.' For Him to give us a glimpse of what is real, of what is truly important, what is enduring and what will still be there for us when the pain of the moment becomes the memory of the past.

Another quote from my journal:

> 'We should be like that "weaned child" in Psalm 131. Totally, absolutely content, asleep on its mother's breast and in the safety and warmth of her arms. No cares, no worries about tomorrow. Just totally at peace and trusting absolutely in our parent's ability to look after us, to cherish and nurture us. Out of that sense of peace and trust will come the "doing" – going where God sends us, doing what He asks us to do. All the rest is striving.'

Do not live in the past – what's gone has gone. You will never completely forget it, of course, but try not to dwell on it. Live one day at a time and within that day, take time out to experience the moment. Whenever you feel the panic and the worry rising, take a few deep breaths, go outside, and focus on what is around you. Hear the birds in the trees, look at the shapes in the clouds, the green of the grass or the blue of the sky and the light sparkling in puddles.

Ask God to show you things during the course of the day. I found this entry in my journal:

> 'This morning I asked God to reveal Himself, asked for just one moment of joy and an awareness of His presence. Later in the day I emerged from the supermarket in the late afternoon. It was almost, but not quite dark and there was something slightly eerie about the light. The whole sky seemed to be lit by this amazing full moon, so clear, so yellow, so round, so perfect, just hanging there in the sky. I had a sense of the awesomeness of God, the God for whom nothing is impossible – a sense of His faithfulness, His absolute loyalty and reliability.
>
> Coming out of that mundane supermarket with my trolley full of bags I caught a glimpse of something; someone bigger than anything the Universe has to offer, a sense of the immortal and infinite, the bigger picture. A

truly incredible moment in the middle of a dark, depressing winter's day.'

True joy is to be discovered, not when everything is going right in our lives, but when everything seems to have gone pear-shaped: When we notice the beauty in the unexpected place of pain – it is in this moment that we experience true joy; Where we discover a God who 'prepares a table for us in the presence of our enemies'. A God who wants us to step aside, out of the worry and the fear and the regret, and become aware of the moment and the world that He has created for us to enjoy; a God who wants us to become aware of Him always walking at our side. These are the times when we are truly alive – the times when somehow we are in touch with the present moment and eternity at the same time.

My Dear Friend:
How are you? I just had to send you this letter to tell you how much I love and care about you. I saw you yesterday as you were walking with your friends. I waited all day, hoping that soon you'd want Me to walk along with you, too.

As evening drew near, I painted you a sunset to close your day and whispered a cool breeze to refresh you, and I waited. You never came. Oh yes, it hurt Me, but I just kept on loving you.

As I watched you fall asleep last night, I longed to touch your brow. I spilled moonlight upon your face, trickling down your cheeks as so many tears have. Again I waited, but you didn't even think of Me. I wanted so much to rush down so we could talk. I have so many gifts for you.

The next day I exploded a brilliant sunrise into glorious morning for you. But you awakened late and rushed off for the day. You didn't even notice Me. My sky became cloudy and My tears were the rain. Oh, how I LOVE YOU!

Today you looked so sad and so alone. It makes My heart ache because I understand. My friends let Me down and hurt Me many times too. Oh, if you'd only listen. I really

LOVE you. I try to say it in the quiet of the green meadow and in the vibrant blue sky. The wind whispers My love throughout the treetops and spills it into the vivid colors of all the flowers. I shout it to you in the in the thunder of the great waterfalls, in mountain streams, and I compose love songs for birds to sing for you.

I warm you with the clothing of My warm sunshine and perfume the air with nature's sweet scent. My love for you is deeper than any ocean and greater than the biggest want or need you may have. If you'd only realise how much I really care.

We will spend eternity together in heaven. I know how hard it is on earth. I know because I was once there. I really want to help you.

My Father cares for you and wants to help you, too. Fathers are just that way. So please, call on Me soon. Just call Me, ask Me, talk to Me. It is your decision. I have chosen you. No matter how long it takes, I'll wait forever because I LOVE YOU!

Your friend,
Jesus   (Author unknown)

Checklist

- Remind yourself, during the course of the day, to 'stop, look and listen', to experience the moment and become aware of the presence of a loving God.

Chapter 12

Acceptance

'. . . for I have learned to be content in all circumstances.'
(Philippians 4:11, RSV)

As time goes by the pain will lessen; however, the process of recovery is not a linear one; you may feel positive for weeks, then something happens – you bump into your ex-partner, you hear something about them, or it's your wedding anniversary and BANG! There you are again, back in that place you thought you'd left behind, back in the mud and the mire with the feelings of sadness, anger, blame, all threatening to pull you under again. But those feelings will be temporary and not as deeply painful as they were at the beginning.

How long will it take?

We are individual and some people will take longer to heal than others. Your personality, the circumstances of your breakdown, the length of your marriage, whether there are children involved; all these things will determine how long it takes to recover.

Too quick

If you get over it too quickly then it is likely that you haven't allowed yourself to grieve properly and experience all the painful emotions that come as a part of the recovery package. People have a way of blocking out pain which may appear to allow them to function normally, to move on, but in reality the seething mess of emotion has been squashed into a box with the lid firmly clamped shut. They harden themselves, tell themselves that they will not allow anyone to come that close again (close enough to hurt them) and it will affect their way of relating to other people. From time to time, that messy blob of emotion they shoved in the box will escape, pouring out uncontrollably and destructively over everything.

Too slow

If, on the other hand, you are still deeply grieving for your marriage several years later, you haven't let go. You cannot move into the future with your feet stuck in the mud of the past, and in order to move forward you have to let go of all what has gone before. There is a time for everything, a 'time to mourn and a time to dance', a 'time to weep and a time to laugh'. Recognise when your time of weeping and mourning are over, when it's time to let go and move on. Mike Riddell puts it this way:

> 'One of the worst possible reactions (though understandable) is to seek to hold onto that which is slipping away from us. It is as futile as gathering snow on a mountaintop to take home in order to have a souvenir of the experience. We have all met people (and may even have been them) who are stuck at some point in their journey because of a refusal to let go and move on. That which we cling to becomes corrupted because of our attachment to it, not to mention the damage done to our own souls. It is necessary to learn to allow the river of life to flow through us, and not to cause it to become stagnant. The desire to clutch handholds in order to resist the current is ultimately self-defeating. As Jesus is reputed to have said, 'Those who try to hold onto their life will lose it.'[25]

If it is several years since the breakdown of your marriage, take the decision to put it down to experience now, let go of the past and move on. We all acquire scars as we go through life. Say, *'C'ést la vie'*, and let it go. Life is for living. By allowing yourself to get stuck in the mire of bitterness and overwhelming sadness, you are missing all that life, and God, has to offer you right now: at this very moment, you are not free. Referring back to an earlier chapter, you need to forgive and to let go of him or her and your marriage, and by doing so you will be loosing yourself from the chains that are holding you back. You may have got stuck somewhere on the way, somewhere in the process of grief and recovery, and you may need counselling to help you see the point where you stopped moving forward – the point you need to return to in order to deal with things and move on.

So, how long?

Depending on the length of the marriage and the circumstances, it will take at least two to three years to be anywhere near recovered. Even then, there will be times when the past comes back to smack you in the face, but as long as the feelings are getting weaker and less frequent over time, you can be assured that you are on the road to recovery. During those times when you wonder whether you'll ever get over it, read through your journal (if you have kept one) to see how far you have come. I found this entry in my journal, written a year after my marriage ended,

> 'I have come a long way in a year; somehow or other I've got from there to here and looking back, I can see that God has been with me every step of the way, though for much of the time I was unaware of his presence in the darkness. He's got me this far and I can trust him to guide me the rest of the way.'

Resignation comes before acceptance. Resignation is when we realise that we cannot change history; what has happened has happened and we just have to make the best of things and get on with life without our partner. We have come to terms with the end of our marriage.

Acceptance comes when we begin not only to endure our single state, but to enjoy it too, if only now and again. Learning to enjoy living alone, or at least learning to be without a husband or wife, is a gradual process. It comes with time. Whether married or single, there are advantages and disadvantages. Cast your mind back and remind yourself of those times in your marriage when you were not blissfully happy. The past was a mixture of good and bad, happy times and miserable times. One thing you can be sure of – the future will be a mixture too.

Losing the plot

Even though you are well along the road to recovery, there will be days when you lose the plot: days when you want to hide behind the settee and hope the world will go away. My 'losing the plot days' usually coincide with something going wrong; the central heating has packed up or I've crashed my car and I've got to deal with it all on my own. On these days I feel angry that my ex-husband isn't there for me, as he was there for twenty-nine years. I'm angrier that he isn't there for me because he's busy being there for someone else.

And then there is the whole dreadful business of getting divorced. It is impossible, until you have the crucial bit of paper in your hand, to be free of the other person while you are still married to them, in law if in no other way. There will still be evenings when you sit alone in front of the TV feeling sorry for yourself, in 'nobody loves me' mode.

Make sure you balance time spent alone with time spent with other people, as prolonged isolation is no good for anyone. Make sure that you're with someone on those all-important days – Christmas and anniversaries – when you'll be feeling the pain of loss more acutely. There will be milestones along the way – the Decree Nisi, the Decree Absolute, moving house. In my case moving house was a huge milestone. As I prepared to move from the marital home into my own house, I was forced to look through drawers, cupboards and wardrobes, forced to sit down and sort through twenty-nine years worth of memories: souvenirs of happy family holidays long past, anniversary cards professing everlasting and undying love, photographs, so many memories. I threw a lot away, a liberating experience, freeing myself from the past. But I kept some things. It's impossible to erase twenty-nine years and I realised that I had come to the point, two-and-a-half years on, where the memories were no longer so painful; a place where I could look back and think, 'Yes, that was a wonderful holiday' and be grateful that I'd shared that experience with my ex-husband; a place where I could be grateful for the love, the closeness and the intimacy of a marriage, even if that marriage had now come to an end.

On your bad days, reach out to people and tell them how you're feeling. Your real friends will be there for you. Avoid like the plague those people who think you 'should be over it'. Odds on, they won't have experienced what you're going through.

Rebuilding

As acceptance comes, begin to rebuild your life. You may have to look for a job or move house so concentrate on those things. You may have to rebuild your social circle. You have an opportunity now to decide what you want for your future. Decide what you want (make those lists) and then take steps to achieve it, steps towards the kind of future you want and the future that God has already mapped out for you. You don't have to try to make the changes all at once, just start with one small thing. God will guide your steps providing you're moving your feet. Nothing will happen if you don't move, if you stand still. Trust in Him to close any doors He doesn't want you to go through. You still need to be moving though, to be going somewhere, or else you'll be paralysed with fear and indecision. God can steer a moving vehicle but it's up to you to turn on the ignition!

Try a spot of lateral thinking; stop being so sensible and practical (if you are), and experiment with thinking 'outside the box'. As Jane Fonda said, this kind of experience can allow us to push doors we would never have thought of opening. There will be a moment at some point in the future when you think, 'I could never have imagined in my wildest dreams being here, doing this, with these people.'

Nurture your relationship with God, for He is your best friend. Put your future in His very capable hands. You're still on the same journey through life, it's just that you've changed direction; you're taking an unexpected route, with all kinds of surprises on the way.

Realise that this is a period of recuperation and recovery. As acceptance comes, you will regain your equilibrium, your peace. It is a slow process, but don't be too impatient, and expect it to take time. Rest assured that God has plans for your future, plans you could not even begin to imagine. The future is bright.

'To long for everything: sorrow; to accept everything: joy.'
(Indian proverb)

'When God shuts one door, he opens another.'
(Arabian proverb)

Checklist

- Acceptance comes gradually, over time.

- Recovery may come too quickly, meaning you have not dealt with issues.

- Recovery may come too slowly, meaning that you have 'got stuck' somewhere in the process of grieving.

- Realise that as long as the painful feelings are becoming weaker over time, you are on the road to recovery.

- Expect to have days when you lose the plot.

- As acceptance comes, begin to rebuild you life. Think about what you want for your future and take steps to achieve the kind of future you want.

- Nurture your relationship with God and trust Him with your future.

Chapter 13

New Relationships

'He heals the brokenhearted
and binds up their wounds.'
(Psalm 147:3)

In the aftermath of a marriage breakdown some people desperately seek a replacement to fill the void left by the departed marriage partner. It can be a form of escapism along the lines of, 'If I can fall in love with someone, they will make everything alright, I'll get married again and live happily ever after and I won't have to think about all this horrible stuff.' Or we have become so accustomed to being married, to belonging to another person, that the prospect of singleness is terrifying to the extreme.

Finding your self-esteem

If you have been left in favour of someone else, you will be feeling the pain of rejection very acutely, and your self-esteem will probably be at an all-time low. Take some time out to discover your own worth, so that your self-esteem comes from within and is not dependent on you belonging to, or being attached to, someone. A person who is confident on their own and at peace with their own identity is much more attractive to others than a needy person, reaching out desperately for almost anyone to fill the gap. That confidence will come in time. Be patient with yourself and endeavour to make the best of this period of solitude, to 'be content in all circumstances'. This time of being alone is a painful but necessary part of the healing process. We human beings have a tendency to rush on ahead of God and land ourselves with all manner of problems in the process. Why run the risk of another broken relationship, with even more pain and rejection to heap burning coals onto your already fragile ego? Why subject another human being to your neediness, your insecurities, and your desperation? Instead of looking frantically for another person to fill the void, lean heavily on God at this time, trusting in Him to get you through, to provide you with your every need, to provide you with human contact and maybe one day, another marriage partner – when *He* thinks you are ready. As my counsellor said to me, 'Get happy being on your own then if a new marriage partner comes along, it will be a bonus.'

It's an easy thing to say and it sounds glib I know – but work towards finding your sense of self-worth in the fact that you are a unique and beautiful individual created by Almighty God, rather than in your status as one half of a couple. You are not one half of anything, but a complete individual. It's a hard lesson for us to learn, particularly when we're lonely and hurting, but we come into this world alone and we go out of it alone. Many people travel through life alone, never experiencing the closeness and intimacy of marriage. At least we have had the experience that's denied to many, even if it didn't last for a lifetime. We don't own people; they belong to one person only and that is God. Yes, we have made promises to one another and we should endeavour to keep them, and we have every right to expect the other person to honour them, but we all have free will and we all break promises.

Recently, a single friend, now in her forties, said to me that she hadn't had the experience of marriage, which is a source of regret and sadness to her, but at the same time, she hadn't had to go through the pain of divorce either. That is looking for the positive! Try to be someone who sees the glass as half full rather than half empty.

I am not going to pretend that singleness is a wonderful state. I have days (lots of them) when I wish there was someone there to share things with. Friends are wonderful, but having friends is not quite the same as having someone who is always there, to whom you have made a special kind of commitment. And on a purely practical level, it's good to have someone to share the household bills with, to go on holiday with, to share the burdens and joys of everyday life. But I must wait. As I write, there is no potential partner in my life.

Dating

I am aware that there are those within the Church who believe that divorced Christians shouldn't remarry (even if adultery was the cause of the marriage breakdown and they were the innocent party), at least until the death of the previous marriage partner. For this reason Christians should apparently not get involved in the kind of relationships that might eventually lead to marriage. In other words, divorced Christians should not date. Well, everyone is entitled to his or her own opinion but I don't subscribe to it, and if you hold this opinion perhaps you'd better skip this section!

It took me about a year, but eventually I popped my head over the parapet to see if there was anyone out there. At the time I was still hurting badly, my emotions were still raw and messy, my confidence was at rock bottom and I was lonely. I wanted to matter to someone, wanted a 'significant other' in my life. I thought, 'Help, I must find someone *soon* or be doomed to a lonely old age.' So I dived over the parapet, dated several men, had a few months' relationship with one or two of them and came out of those relationships feeling much worse than when I went into them. Relationships require time, energy, effort and commitment, and I wasn't ready for that kind of commitment; I was still trying to cope with the emotional fallout and the practical processes of becoming unmarried. I also discovered that some of these men had problems of their own which they hadn't worked through; that maybe they hadn't come to terms with their own marriage breakdowns and that they were in no fit state to enter into a committed, loving relationship with another woman.

Desperation

Loneliness can cause us to behave in ways that smack of desperation, and desperation is never attractive. Desperation can be absolutely terrifying to potential suitors. I know – I've been at both ends of the spectrum, the desperate one and also one at the receiving end of desperation. Neither is a good place to be.

Desperation will have you investing far too much in a relationship, too early on. So that, a few weeks or months down the line, if things don't work out and the other person decides you aren't the one for them, you are left with a profound sense of rejection. The other person may have decided that you are a perfectly nice person, but not the one they want to spend the rest of their life with. However, because of your history, you can perceive this as yet another rejection of everything that you are – of your entire being.

Anger

If you are still angry with your ex-partner, that anger may spill out into your new liaison. You may find yourself getting angry with the other person when the anger should really be directed at your ex (or preferably, dispensed with altogether – but we're all human). This is misdirected anger and it is as though in your less rational moments, the other person must pay for the pain you have gone through.

Or you may find yourself at the receiving end of seemingly irrational anger that is undeserved, but it is the consequence of your new partner's anger against his or her previous spouse and nothing at all to do with you.

Mistrust

Maybe there is an issue of mistrust. If your spouse betrayed you, you may be half expecting your new partner to betray you too, so you are constantly suspicious and always on your guard. And there is much truth, I think, in the saying, 'We get what we expect.'

It's so much pain that no wonder God requires us to work through the difficulties of marriage and commit to each other, no matter what, in good times and in bad times. Essentially, this loving God of ours wants to spare us unnecessary agony.

Baggage handling

It is almost inevitable that we will find ourselves in a relationship with someone who has been through a divorce or bereavement; so there are two sets of baggage, theirs and ours. No wonder second marriages are far more likely to fail than first marriages statistically. This must be, in part, because too many people rush into a new relationship. A new relationship can be a form of pain-avoidance, a means of making us feel better, and for a while it works. But what happens when the initial heady romance wears off and real life sets in, with all its distractions and boring routine? It is likely that the issues we have not dealt with (the painful feelings we've pushed down) will emerge and sour our new relationship. Or our buttons get pressed and off we go on the spiral again, reacting in all the same old ways that played havoc with our previous relationships.

We need to be aware of the reasons for our reactions and seek to make changes: to learn from the mistakes of the past, to be aware of our vulnerabilities, our weak spots and the places where we are still hurting. In order to do this we need a good, long period of reflection; we need to ask ourselves what went wrong in our marriages – how we could have reacted differently, how we could have avoided the mistakes? This is a wonderful God-given opportunity to re-evaluate our lives and decide what we want. By diving back into a one-to-one relationship too soon we are denying ourselves the opportunity to change things long term.

How would you feel if you attracted someone who was grieving and still angry? Someone who couldn't give you their full attention because they still have one foot firmly stuck in the past? Don't do it to another person. Work through the process of grief and anger first. You may want a new relationship because you can't bear to be alone, but would you really want a relationship with someone who is with you *only because they can't bear being alone*?

You have to be with someone because you like being with that person, not because you want to avoid loneliness or want to be married again. You should enjoy spending time with them, with that particular person, not just because their presence fills up the lonely evenings and weekends as that's just using the other person. You would want someone to be with you because they really liked you and wanted to be with you; you wouldn't want them to be using you to fill up the lonely hours. Do unto others what you would have them do unto you!

When going into a new relationship, try to keep your eyes wide open. Rebound relationships can fulfil a purpose but hold onto them lightly – realise the difficulties that exist and realise that you may not be *compos mentis* at the moment.

With any new relationship try to have no expectations, just take things one day at a time. Don't expect one person to fill the void and to make you happy. The responsibility to make you happy does not rest with other people – it rests entirely with you.

Sex

This is a difficult issue, especially if you have been married for many years and have been used to sex being a regular and intrinsic part of your life. Suddenly it's not there any more and it's very difficult to switch off what is a God-given part of our physical and emotional make-up – our sexuality.

I hope I am not going to come over all preachy or patronising. The following observations are mostly just plain common sense.

To sleep around is very clearly *not* a good idea. There's no love and there's no respect, either for each other or for yourself. In your loneliness and your desperation you give everything away to someone you hardly know, and in the process you demean and cheapen yourself. In the aftermath of marriage breakdown many people sleep around (even Christians). Secular books I've read on the subject of relationship breakdown often tell their readers to go out and have as much sex as possible in order to eradicate feelings of rejection and loss, to make themselves feel desirable and attractive, to build their ego and also to build a barrier between them and their former spouse. However, sleeping around is not the answer; it does not lead to happiness and peace.

Casual sex is a no-no, but what if you've met someone very special. What if this person could be *the* one?

Sex takes a relationship onto a deeper level. You have made yourself very vulnerable, you become more involved emotionally, and another layer is added, along with a different and more complex set of expectations. What if things don't work out? What if it becomes patently obvious a little further down the line that this is not a match made in heaven?

I have a friend who refuses to sleep with her boyfriend on the grounds that if she does so, and the relationship later evaporates, she will be left with a feeling of having compromised her standards; of having let herself and God down, of being left with one more thing to repent of, and of being another step down on the Self-Respect Ladder. It will be one more thing to beat herself up with.

It's to do with self-respect and also self-preservation. You have been through quite enough already – why subject yourself to even more emotional pain? Why make yourself even more vulnerable by having sex with someone, with all that it entails in terms of your emotions? Sex is not a cheap commodity; it's not something to be given away as though it has no value. And for women in particular, sex is much more than just the physical act – the emotions are involved too. Sex is something that should be part of a fully-committed, loving relationship.

It's to do with taking control, and by saying 'no' you are being assertive, valuing yourself, taking control of your life and building confidence. When it becomes obvious that this person is not going to be a permanent fixture, it's much easier to pull back and walk away if you haven't slept with them.

One last word on the subject: if you are someone for whom this advice has come a bit too late, or if you knew it all along but chose to ignore it ... please don't beat yourself up about it. The Bible tells us that sex outside marriage is a sin, and any sin will drive a wedge between our heavenly Father and us – but all sin can be forgiven.

Relationships are messy and unpredictable things. Human beings are messy and unpredictable too. God knew you were going to mess up ... but He chose you anyway.

Biding your time

New post-divorce relationships can be fraught with difficulties and rather than leaping headlong in there, it's better to bide your time and wait until you are further along the road to recovery; until you are less needy and vulnerable. Concentrate on *you*, and on rebuilding your life. Fill the void by building up a network of supportive friends – by working on your social life, and finding new interests and hobbies. This is your time; a time to rebuild and to make changes for the better. There will come a day when you are ready to find someone new, a day when you have worked through the pain and when you will have something to give back.

I remember reading somewhere that 95% of people who are presently single will, in two years' time, be in a relationship and that if they knew that now, they'd be out partying every night! A very positive note on which to end this chapter, I feel!

'If grass can grow through cement, love can find you at every time in your life.'   (Cher)[26]

'Love has nothing to do with what you are expecting to get, it's what you are expected to give – which is everything.'   (Anon)

'Immature love says: "I love you because I need you." Mature love says: "I need you because I love you."'
(Erich Fromm)[27]

Checklist

- It is unwise to start a new relationship while still grappling with the painful aftermath of separation and divorce.

- When you feel ready for a new relationship be aware of the potential problems.

- Think hard before becoming involved in a sexual relationship.

Chapter 14

The Ripples on the Lake

'My friends and companions avoid me because of my wounds;
my neighbours stay far away.'
(Psalm 38:11)

'I pray to you tonight, Lord,
   for Marcel and for her
   and for the other one
   and for the wife of the other one
   and for his children
   and for the families involved
   and for the neighbours who gossip
   and for the colleagues who judge.'
(Michel Quoist)[28]

Even after the storm has abated, the ripples go on. A marriage breakdown affects many more people than just the two at the centre of the storm. There are the children, the parents of the couple, the friends and work colleagues, sisters and brothers and, if one partner left the other for another married person, there is a whole other set of people who are grieving – another family torn apart. Many relationships will change for better or worse, including your relationship with God.

In-laws

The parents of the previously married couple are deeply affected by the marriage breakdown. Overnight they may lose a daughter-in-law or a son-in-law who they have come to love and regard as one of their own children. And if there are grandchildren involved there may be issues to do with access. They may no longer see their grandchildren as often as they did before.

If you had a good relationship with your in-laws, you find that you have lost a large part of your family and support structure. The in-laws may side with their offspring; they are probably hearing only one side of the story and it is almost inevitable and natural that in an acrimonious divorce situation they will support their child.

When my husband's father died, not long after my husband left me, I had great difficulty in coming to terms with the fact that it was my 'replacement' who was at the bedside with my husband and the assembled family, and not me. I loved my father-in-law, I had known him for thirty-five years, and he had a big impact on my life, yet I was aware that my presence would cause awkwardness at the hospital bedside. Visits had to be timed carefully to avoid my husband and his new partner. It was *her* who was there at the end, although she had known him for such a short time, when I would have liked to be there to be with him and to lend comfort to my mother-in-law. I felt as though I had been 'ousted'. I was no longer a member of the family legally, although my lovely mother-in-law assured me that I would always be a part of the family in her heart, and I would always be the mother of her grandchildren. It seemed as though I had lost not only my husband, but also my parents-in-law, my brothers and sisters-in-law and the wider family members. It seemed strange that my children were members of that family by virtue of their parentage and their surname, but that I, however irrational the notion, seemed to have been erased, rubbed out.

Early on, I would occasionally pop round to see my parents-in-law but found the experience too painful. Either they would refer, as is perfectly natural, to their son (who had been my husband), dropping into the conversation that he'd done this or that. Or, horror of horrors and forgetting themselves for a moment, they would refer in passing to something my husband's new partner had done or said. Or they would studiously avoid the mention of his name, which seemed unnatural. The whole experience of being in their home, which normally I would have visited with my husband, of seeing the family photos on display, even of seeing the physical resemblance between my parents-in-law and my husband, was too much for me to cope with. I decided that my well-being was paramount and that I needed to take a break from visiting, much as I loved them. I hoped that they would understand. I'm not sure that they did understand, especially at first, but rather were hurt instead.

Remember that whether they understand is not your responsibility and that provided you have tried to explain why you find visits difficult, you have done all you can. If you can't face the in-laws then explain to them how you're feeling. Later on, you may feel that you want to start visiting again. It is imperative that if you have young children, you ensure that they continue to have contact with their grandparents regularly, even if you cannot face visits yourself.

Children

So far I have not mentioned the effect of a marriage breakdown on any children of the relationship. Obviously the effects are profound, but can be minimised by sensitive handling. It will not be easy however, at a time when your emotions are unstable and when you are trying to cope with the practicalities of daily life, and perhaps also, the process of divorce.

The subject of children and divorce is a huge one and there is not room enough in this book to cover all aspects. However, there are many excellent books available on the subject.

Reassurance

At this time of upheaval and uncertainty, children need as much reassurance as you can muster. When parents split up a child's whole world is turned upside down. If you are the one who left and the other partner has custody of the children, make every effort to see them often. Keep access appointments come what may, and be punctual. They need to know that you are there for them, despite your absence in the family home.

If you are the one with custody of the children, ensure that they know you are not going to disappear too. It might seem obvious, but children feel even less in control of things than you, and live with a very real fear of abandonment. There will be a sense of having been rejected by the parent who has left so give them as much extra time and attention as you are able.

They will want to know what the practical implications are – whether they will have to move house, where you will be living, whether they will have to go to another school, the implications of financial constraints and so on. Maybe if you were previously at home caring for the children, you will have to go out to work. This will be another change that the children will have to learn to cope with and they need to be prepared as much as possible.

Essentially, it's important to remember that the children are grieving too and will, in their own way, be going through the same distressing process as you; the shock, the denial, the anger, the guilt. They will take time to heal, so be patient with them. Many children take on the responsibility for the breakdown, feeling that if they had behaved better, their parents would still be together. Do all in your power to rid them of this notion.

Stability and routine

The insecurity that comes with the breakdown of a parent's marriage is very frightening and unsettling to a child – children need routine and stability in their lives. They need to continue seeing friends and relatives and being involved in their usual interests and activities. They also need the routine and discipline of daily life. There is perhaps, a tendency to loosen up on discipline, but children need to know where the boundaries are in order to feel safe and secure.

For a time, their behaviour at school may be affected; they may become naughty, or withdrawn. Keep the teachers informed of the major changes that are going on at home so that he or she will understand and treat your child accordingly.

Enlist the help of the wider family network. Grandparents, aunts and uncles, as well as the parents of your children's friends, may be able to spend time with them, giving them a sense of stability and of ordinary family life going on. Perhaps it will also give them an opportunity to talk, while at the same time give you some much-needed space.

Speak positively

This will be a difficult one, but no matter how tempting, and no matter how angry or how betrayed you may be feeling, try hard not to jeopardise your children's relationship with your ex by according blame and by venting your wrath in front of them. Most of all, do not use your children as an 'emotional football', a means of getting back at your ex-partner by denying access or trying to 'get them on your side'. It's easier said than done. Try not to speak negatively about your ex, no matter how much anger may be churning round in you. Assure your children that the other parent still loves them deeply and will always be there for them. When you are together with the children present, take a deep breath and try to be as civil as possible, saving any possible disagreements until another time.

Adult children

Adult children suffer every bit as much as young children when their parents split up. In my own case, my children were twenty-one and twenty-six when the breakdown occurred.

My husband's brother had left his wife and two children three months previously, and the reaction of other family members to the two sets of circumstances was interesting. My young niece and nephew received lots of attention from uncles, aunts and grandparents, as is only right and proper. Family members, however, considered my two children to be grown up and well able to cope with the situation, but parental separation can be just as profoundly upsetting for older children as for younger ones – it's just different.

I am thankful that I did not have to endure what my sister-in-law went through, having her children wave goodbye as they trotted off with their father to spend time with him and his new partner, then being regaled on their return with the minutiae of their father's new life and relationship. Oodles of grace needed, I think. I'm so grateful that I didn't have to see my husband on a regular basis, calling to collect his children. Our children were living elsewhere, having long flown the nest. I always tried to encourage them to keep in contact with their father, even when they didn't want to have anything to do with him, and everything in me wanted them to be on my side and not speak to him!

You owe it not only to yourself, but to your children too, to become a happy, stable, fulfilled person again. Your children will be worried about you and will respond to your general mood. They will adjust and learn to cope with the new situation as they see you recovering and becoming a happier person.

Relationships change

To one extent or another, most or all of your relationships will undergo change at this time. Hopefully, your friends will rally round and support you. Some will become closer as they seek to help you and provide a listening ear.

Sadly, some friendships may evaporate altogether, either because these people no longer know how to relate to you now that you are single, or maybe because they don't know what to do or say, and so avoid you. Friends who have known you only as half of a married couple may 'take sides' and come down on the side of your ex-partner. You may find the invitations drying up from friends who knew you as 50% of a couple, as you will not be so easy to place around a dinner table. At this time, you will find your single friends invaluable as a support network.

Your relationship with God

Your relationship with God will change too. You may become closer to God; certainly He will become closer to you.

'The LORD is close to the brokenhearted
and saves those who are crushed in spirit.'   (Psalm 34:18)

At this time you need to lean heavily on Him and allow Him to support and carry you. Essentially, this is what this book has been about.

Sadly, some people will gradually lose their faith and drift away from the Church and from God. They may feel disappointed in God for allowing this catastrophe to happen. Or they may feel a deep sense of failure, of having failed in their marriage and of letting God down.

As we travel through life we will all hit stormy waters at some point, and these are the times of testing. It's easy to walk with God when everything is going right in our lives, but when troubles come (as they come to everyone) that's when we discover whether we are truly rooted in God. Remember the parable of the farmer sowing seed:

> *'Listen! A farmer went out to sow his seed. As he was scattering the seed, some fell along the path, and the birds came and ate it up. Some fell on rocky places, where it did not have much soil. It sprang up quickly, because the soil was shallow. But when the sun came up, the plants were scorched, and they withered because they had no root. Other seed fell among thorns, which grew up and choked the plants, so that they did not bear grain. Still other seed fell on good soil. It came up, grew and produced a crop, multiplying thirty, sixty, or even a hundred times.'*
> (Mark 4:3–8)

There are many who will not make it, many who will fall away from God because everything seems to have gone wrong in their lives, because the marriage they considered to be a gift from God has died.

Do we love God because He gives us good things, because He answers our prayers? This is a shallow, immature kind of love that will not survive the trials and tribulation of life. Or, do we love Him for who He is, in spite of everything that may happen to us in our lives? If that is the case then we are truly rooted

(Ephesians 3:17 says that we are rooted in love). Don't be one of those who allow disappointment to snatch away the most important relationship of all.

Looking back through my journals I realise quite an amazing thing. At those times when I felt furthest away from God – when I felt most bereft and depressed, when I felt as though the boat had been cut adrift and was crashing against the rocks and when God seemed far away and out of hearing range – these were the times when I was closest to Him, and He to me. It is only in retrospect that I can see it.

> 'One night a man had a dream. He dreamt he was walking along a beach with the Lord. Across the sky flashed scenes from his life. For each scene he noticed two sets of footprints in the sand: one belonging to him and the other to the Lord. When the last scene of his life flashed before him, he looked back at the footprints in the sand. He noticed that many times along the path of his life there was only one set of footprints. He also noticed that it happened at the very lowest and saddest times in his life. This really bothered him and he questioned the Lord about it.
>
> "Lord, you said that once I decided to follow You, You'd walk with me all the way. But I have noticed that during the most troublesome times in my life, there is only one set of footprints. I don't understand that when I needed You most, You would leave me."
>
> The Lord replied, "My precious child, I love you and I would never leave you. During your times of trial and suffering when you see only one set of footprints, it was then that I carried you." (Anon.)

Church

People may become disillusioned with church, especially if the support they so desperately need is not forthcoming, and they may drift away on a tide of disappointment and rejection. Hopefully, your church will support you at this time. On the whole, mine did. But a church consists of a collection of human beings with human frailties, and it is perhaps inevitable that there will be those among your church friends who will not provide the level of support you need. Do not allow any resentment to colour your relationship with your church. Many people will just not have the faintest idea what you are going through and may seem unsympathetic. Despite the fact that divorce is so prevalent in our society, unless people have been through the experience themselves, they will only have limited understanding of what you are going through. I think that there is often much more sympathy for bereaved people than for those who are negotiating the process of divorce, although the process is similar and can be (I believe) worse. In no way do I wish to belittle the devastating experience of bereavement. However, when a marriage partner dies, they die still loving you. When a marriage partner leaves you, especially if they leave you in favour of someone else, that person has withdrawn their love and rejected you. That person is still alive and has chosen someone else over and above you, so there is not only grief at the ending of the marriage, but also rejection and humiliation to cope with.

Sadly, you may find that your new status within the church changes the way others perceive you. You may find yourself being gently dropped from some of your previous functions, or you will not be asked to do things. This may be a deliberate act of kindness, to allow you space at this difficult time, allowing you time to heal. As you recover, you may find that others have filled your place; that invitations to serve are no longer forthcoming. It seems as though some churches are uncomfortable with single people and would much prefer a congregation composed entirely of cosy couples.

I have spoken to divorced people who changed the church they attended, wanting to go to a church where they would be known and valued as a single person, where people wouldn't remember them as one half of a couple. I think that this is a perfectly valid desire and, providing you have prayed about it and feel that if it is a right move and not just a desire to run away, it can be a useful part of the healing process and another step along the way to recovery.

> 'Write the bad things that are done to you in sand, but write the good things that happen to you on a piece of marble.' (Arabic parable)

Checklist

- Realise that many relationships will change, for better or worse.

- If visiting the in-laws upsets you, explain to them and withdraw, if only for a while.

- Give children as much reassurance as you can. Recognise that they too, are grieving.

- Keep children informed of the practical implications.

- Maintain routine and discipline in the children's lives.

- Try not to do anything to jeopardise the children's relationship with the other partner.

- Realise that adult children are suffering too.

- Most important of all, maintain your relationship with God and draw close to Him.

Chapter 15

The Calm After the Storm

*'Now to him who is able to do immeasurably more than we ask
or imagine, according to his power that is at work within us,
to him be the glory in the church and in Jesus Christ
throughout all generations, for ever and ever! Amen.'*
(Ephesians 3:20–21)

After the Storm

Lord, I saw the sea attacking the rocks, sombre and raging.
From afar the waves gained momentum.
High and proud they leaped, jostling one another to be the
    first to strike.
When the white foam drew back, leaving the rock clear,
    they gathered themselves to rush forward again.

The other day I saw the sea calm and serene
The waves came from afar, creeping, not to draw attention;
Quietly holding hands, they slipped noiselessly and stretched
    at full length on the sand to touch the shore with the
    tips of their beautiful, mossy fingers.
The sun gently caressed them, and they generously returned
    streams of light.
              (Michel Quoist, *The Sea*)[29]

However you may be feeling at the moment, there will come a
day when you realise that the past is well and truly behind you

and that you have weathered the storm; a day when you realise that memories no longer have the power to paralyse you. Instead of agonising pain, there is now only a dull ache that, like a soldier's war wound, will twinge from time to time but will no longer cause you long-term discomfort. Only the scar remains.

You will realise that the storm is over, that the sea is calm and that the sun has emerged from behind the clouds. It is useful to remember that your war wound may be different from someone else's and that all human beings acquire a scar or two along the way if they remain on the earth long enough. Business failure may cause people to lose their financial security, livelihood and their homes. Maybe a child dies through illness or accident, or a parent contracts a fatal disease. Some are affected by long-term unemployment, by war, by accidents, or their house goes up in flames. Some go to prison, others are born mentally or physically disabled or perhaps disablement comes later in life. The list is endless – we all have scars.

When the storm has abated you will be looking to the future, maybe with some apprehension, but also with anticipation. You will have made some decisions about your future and will have taken steps to put those decisions into effect. The life change that has been thrust upon you can now be endured and even embraced, and you will be able to glimpse, no matter how hazily, the possibilities that lie before you.

By now you will be taking control of your life and will no longer allow life to control you. For a long time I felt as though I was careering downhill on a bike, that I had let go of the handlebars and that everything was out of control. I needed to stop being a victim of circumstances, grab the handlebars and take command of my vehicle. I'm grateful that during this time God was steering the bike and I didn't crash at the bottom of the hill.

Ultimately, the only expectation that you can realistically have for your life is that the unexpected will happen. But how well you endure the unexpected, how you will cope with the change, is largely in your hands. Kathleen Norris says:

'None of us knows what the next change is going to be, what unexpected opportunity is just around the corner, waiting a few months or a few years to change all the tenor of our lives.'[30]

Don't forget to ask God to encourage you on a daily basis. So many of us ask for God's blessings for others but forget about ourselves. Like a human parent, God loves to give gifts to His children – we just don't ask enough. Sometimes He gives us those gifts anyway, but other times He likes us to ask, and waits for us to tell Him what we want. Every day, soon after you wake, thank God for another day and ask Him to encourage you. He will. Pray the prayer of Jabez:

'Jabez cried out to the God of Israel, "Oh, that you would bless me and enlarge my territory! Let your hand be with me, and keep me from harm so that I will be free from pain." And God granted his request.'   (1 Chronicles 4:10)

Jabez didn't go on to do marvellous deeds. He is not noted for anything other than praying that God would bless him. So why is it there in the Bible, amongst all the reports of people performing wonderful deeds for God? Maybe God wants to remind us to ask. He blessed Jabez and He will bless you too.

Counting

There comes a point where you stop counting. At the beginning you count the days (twenty-seven days since we split up), then you count the weeks (five weeks since we split up), then the months, then the years. And then one day, someone will ask you when your marriage broke up and you'll have to work it out 'Errrmm, two years and ... five months' or 'Four years – I think!' At that point – the point where you no longer have it committed to memory but have to work it out – you'll know that you've reached a huge milestone.

An exciting future

A quote from my journal, written twenty months after my husband left me:

> 'I know that my future holds many things that I cannot, at this moment, imagine or dream of. The future can be likened to the new journal that I'm about to start. Blank and void. I have a choice. I can choose what to write on those empty pages. I can choose to write down negative, hopeless thoughts. Or I can choose to be positive, despite my circumstances, which although they may seem dreadful to me, are a whole lot better than most people's in the world.
>
> I can choose to greet the world with a sour face and bitter words or alternatively, I can choose to light up my very small part of the world with my very best, most dazzling smile. There is life, and life in abundance waiting for me. And I want it, I choose to accept it with gratefulness, anticipation and open arms.
>
> I will put my hope in God and thank him in advance for the future he has in store for me. A future that will have its ups and its downs. God has brought me through this crisis, he has not let me down and I now know that he will not fail me in the years to come. Whatever happens, whatever crises lie in store, because I have survived this with God's help, I know that he will not fail me.
>
> I will put my hope in God and thank him in advance. There will be good times and bad times and lots of surprises on the way. I will surrender my life to him daily because with him at the centre, everything else will fall into place.'

I arrived at this point in the journey after many, many times of hopelessness – of feeling that my whole world had come crashing down on me; times of anger, of disappointment, blame and hatred, of desperate sadness, and of doubts about the goodness of God. I guess, realistically, there may still be days when all that stuff will come back to smack me in the teeth, but it will be fleeting.

I have emerged, battered and bruised, but still intact, and hopefully a wiser and stronger person: certainly a person who has experienced the overwhelming love of God in a very real and tangible way. I didn't do all of it right and I wasn't this super-spiritual creature floating round on a cloud or in a little holy bubble like a hamster in a plastic ball. Sometimes I did it all wrong; sometimes I doubted the very existence of God and sometimes behaved in a way that was anything but gracious. Sometimes I didn't speak to God for weeks, and sometimes I put other things (people and relationships) before Him. All too often I drifted away from the centre, but like a pendulum attached to a clock – by God's grace – I kept on coming back to the centre. I just bumbled through somehow or other, which is what most of us do. We're all human and God loves us that way, with all our failings and weaknesses. It doesn't matter how far we drift away from Him, how many times we make a mess of things, or how much sin we fall into as He is a God of infinite and incomprehensible grace, who will always be there with open arms to welcome us back, simply because He loves us.

There is a hope and a future, especially if you place that future firmly in God's hands. Have grace with yourself and stop beating yourself around the head with sticks, as you have endured quite enough pain already.

There is joy and laughter, happiness and contentment and *life* and blessings in abundance, waiting for you. You are about to step over a threshold. God is on the other side, in the sunshine, waiting to grab hold of your hand and longing to show you all the good things He has in store for you. This is a new season – a doorway to a new and exciting future.

The Lord bless you and keep you; the Lord make His face to shine upon you; The Lord turn His face towards you and give you peace.

I will leave the (almost) final word to Sonny Carroll ...

The Awakening

There comes a time in your life when you finally get it ...
When in the midst of all your fears and insanity you stop
dead in your tracks and somewhere the voice inside your
head cries out – ENOUGH! Enough fighting and crying or
struggling to hold on. And, like a child quieting down after
a blind tantrum, your sobs begin to subside, you shudder
once or twice, you blink back your tears and through a
mantle of wet lashes you begin to look at the world from a
new perspective. This is your awakening.

You realise that it is time to stop hoping and waiting
for something, or someone, to change or for happiness,
safety and security to come galloping over the next
horizon. You come to terms with the fact that there
aren't always fairytale endings (or beginnings for that
matter) and that any guarantee of 'happily ever after'
must begin with you. Then a sense of serenity is born of
acceptance.

So you begin making your way through the 'reality of
today' rather than holding out for the 'promise of tomorrow'. You realise that much of who you are, and the
way you navigate through life is, in great part, a result of
all the social conditioning you've received over the course
of a lifetime. And you begin to sift through all the
nonsense you were taught about:

- how you should look and how much you should weigh
- what you should wear and where you should shop
- where you should live or what type of car you should
  drive
- who you should sleep with and how you should behave
- who you should marry and why you should stay
- the importance of having children or even what you
  owe your family

Slowly you begin to open up to new worlds and different
points of view. And you begin reassessing and redefining
who you are and what you really believe in. And you begin

to discard the doctrines you have outgrown, or should never have practised to begin with.

You accept the fact that you are not perfect and that not everyone will love, appreciate or approve of who or what you are ... and that's OK ... *they are entitled to their own views and opinions.* And, you come to terms with the fact that you will never be a size 5 or a 'perfect 10' Or a perfect human being for that matter. So you stop trying to compete with the image inside your head or agonising over how you compare. And you take a long look at yourself in the mirror and you make a promise to give yourself the same unconditional love and support you give so freely to others. Then a sense of confidence is born of self-approval.

And, you stop manoeuvring through life merely as a 'consumer' hungry for your next fix, a new dress, another pair of shoes or looks of approval and admiration from family, friends or even strangers who pass by. Then you discover that it is truly in giving that we receive and that the joy and abundance you seek grows out of the giving. And you recognise the importance of 'creating' and 'contributing' rather than 'obtaining' and 'accumulating'.

And you give thanks for the simple things you've been blessed with; things that millions of people upon the face of the earth can only dream about: a full refrigerator, clean running water, a soft warm bed and the freedom to pursue your own dreams.

And then you begin to love and to care for yourself. You stop engaging in self-destructive behaviours including participating in dysfunctional relationships. You begin eating a balanced diet, drinking more water and exercising. And because you've learned that fatigue drains the spirit and creates doubt and fear, you give yourself permission to rest. And just as food is fuel for the body, laughter is fuel for the spirit and so you make it a point to create time for play.

Then you learn about love and relationships, how to

love, how much to give in love, when to stop giving and when to walk away. And you allow only the hands of a lover who truly loves and respects you to glorify you with his touch. You learn that people don't always say what they mean or mean what they say, intentionally or unintentionally and that not everyone will always come through and interestingly enough, it's not always about you. So, you stop lashing out and pointing fingers or looking to place blame for the things that were done to you or weren't done for you. And you learn to keep your Ego in check and to acknowledge and redirect the destructive emotions it spawns; anger, jealousy and resentment.

You learn how to say I was wrong and to forgive people for their own human frailties. You learn to build bridges instead of walls and about the healing power of love as it is expressed through a kind word, a warm smile or a friendly gesture. And, at the same time, you eliminate any relationships that are hurtful or fail to uplift and edify you. You stop working so hard at smoothing things over and setting your needs aside. You learn that feelings of entitlement are perfectly OK and that it is your right to want or expect certain things. And you learn the importance of communicating your needs with confidence and grace. You learn that the only cross to bear is the one you choose to carry and that eventually martyrs are burned at the stake. Then you learn to distinguish between guilt, and responsibility and the importance of setting boundaries and learning to say NO. You learn that you don't know all the answers, it's not your job to save the world and that sometimes you just need to Let Go.

Moreover, you learn to look at people as they really are and not as you would want them to be, and you are careful not to project your neediness or insecurities onto a relationship. You learn that you will not be, more beautiful, more intelligent, more loveable or important because of the man on your arm or the child that bears your name. You learn that just as people grow and change, so it is with love and relationships and that that not everyone can always love you the way you would want them to. So you stop appraising your worth by the measure of love you are given. And suddenly you realise that it's wrong to demand that someone live their life or sacrifice their dreams just to serve your needs, ease your insecurities, or meet 'your' standards and expectations. You learn that the only love worth giving and receiving is the love that is given freely without conditions or limitations. And you learn what it means to love. So you stop trying to control people, situations and outcomes. You learn that 'alone' does not mean 'lonely' and you begin to discover the joy of spending time 'with yourself' and 'on yourself'. Then you discover the greatest and most fulfilling love you will ever know. Self-Love. And so, it comes to pass that through understanding your heart heals; and now all new things are possible.

Moving along, you begin to avoid toxic people and conversations. And you stop wasting time and energy rehashing your situation with family and friends. You learn that talk doesn't change things and that unrequited wishes can only serve to keep you trapped in the past. So, you stop lamenting over what could or should have been and you make a decision to leave the past behind. Then you begin to invest your time and energy to affect positive change. You take a personal inventory of all your strengths and weaknesses and the areas you need to improve in order to move ahead. You set your goals and map out a plan of action to see things through.

You learn that life isn't always fair and you don't always get what you think you deserve and you stop personalising every loss or disappointment. You learn to accept that sometimes bad things happen to good people and that these things are not an act of God ... but merely a random act of fate.

And you stop looking for guarantees because you've learned that the only thing you can really count on is the unexpected and that whatever happens, you'll learn to deal with it. And you learn that the only thing you must truly fear is the great robber baron of all time FEAR itself. So you learn to step right into and through your fears because to give into fear is to give away the right to live life on your terms. You learn that much of life truly is a self-fulfilling prophecy and you learn to go after what you want and not to squander your life living under a cloud of indecision or feelings of impending doom.

Then, YOU LEARN ABOUT MONEY ... the personal power and independence it brings and the options it creates. And you recognise the necessity to create your own personal wealth. Slowly, you begin to take respons-ibility for yourself by yourself and you make yourself a promise to never betray yourself and to never ever settle for less than your heart's desire. Then a sense of power is born of self-reliance. And you live with honour and integrity because you know that these principles are not the outdated ideals of a by-gone era but the mortar that holds together the foundation upon which you must build your life. And you make it a point to keep smiling, to keep trusting and to stay open to every wonderful opportunity and exciting possibility. Then you hang a wind chime outside your window to remind yourself what beauty there is in Simplicity.

Finally, with courage in your heart and with God by your side you take a stand, you FAKE a deep breath and you begin to design the life you want to live as best as you can.

A word about the Power of Prayer: In some of my darkest, most painful and frightening hours, I have prayed not for the answers to my prayers or for material things but for my God to help me find the strength, confidence and courage to persevere; to face each day and to do what I must do.

Remember this: 'You are an expression of the almighty. The spirit of God resides within you and moves through you. Open your heart, speak to that spirit and it will heal and empower you.' My God has never failed me.[31]

And the very, very last word to Jesus ...

> '... He has sent me to bind up the brokenhearted,*
>   *to proclaim freedom for the captives*
>   *and release from darkness for the prisoners,*
> *to proclaim the year of the* LORD's *favour*
>   *and the day of vengeance of our God,*
> *to comfort all who mourn,*
>   *and provide for those who grieve in Zion –*
> *to bestow on them a crown of beauty*
>   *instead of ashes,*
> *the oil of gladness*
>   *instead of mourning,*
> *and a garment of praise*
>   *instead of a spirit of despair* ... '   (Isaiah 61:1–3)

Amen!

Notes

1. Michel Quoist, *Prayers* (Sheed and Ward, 1963, 1991, 1999), p. 54.
2. R.S. Thomas, *Collected Poems 1945–1990* (Pheonix, 2000), p. 517.
3. Barna Research Group (Venture, California), www.barna.org
4. Debbie Then, *Women Who Stay With Men Who Stray* (HarperCollins, 1998).
5. Helen Steiner Rice, *Sunshine of Joy* (Fleming H. Revell, 1968), Helen Steiner Rice Foundation, 1988.
6. Mike Riddell, *Sacred Journey* (Lion Publishing, 2002), p. 32.
7. Mark Twain, *Pudd'nhead Wilson's Calendar* (1894).
8. Julian of Norwich, 1343–c. 1429, *Revelations of Divine Love*.
9. Sonny Carroll, *Fear. The True Prince of Darkness*, www.waketolife.com
10. Ian McEwan, *Enduring Love* (Vintage, 1998).
11. Jeff Lucas, *Walking Backwards. Dealing with Guilt* (Scripture Union, 1997), p. 9.
12. In a letter to the author (2002).
13. Jonathan Larson, *Rent* (William Morrow, 1997).
14. Wendy Cope, *Serious Concerns* (Faber & Faber, 1992).
15. Joan Powers, inspired by A A Milne, *Pooh's Little Instruction Book* (Duttons Books, 1995).
16. Mariella Frostrup, *The Observer Magazine* (8th December, 2002).
17. Phyllis Hobe, *Never Alone* (MacMillan Publishing Company, 1986).
18. Betty Friedan, *The Feminine Mystique* (W.W. Norton and Company, 2001), ch. 14.
19. *The Observer Magazine* (2nd February, 2003).
20. Marcus Aurelius, *Meditations* (Weidenfield and Nicholson, 2003), p. 86.
21. Alexander Pope, *Letter to William Fortescue* (1725).
22. Aldous Huxley, *Texts and Pretexts: An Anthology with Commentaries* (Vintage/Ebury, 1974).

23. Nicholas Chamfort, *Maximes et pensees* (1796).
24. R.S. Thomas, *Collected Poems 1945–1990*, ibid., p. 302.
25. Mike Riddell, *Sacred Journey* (Lion Publishing, 2002), p. 119.
26. Cher, *The Times* (1998).
27. Erich Fromm, *The Art of Loving* (Perennial, 2000), ch. 2.
28. Michel Quoist, *Prayers*, ibid., p. 54.
29. Ibid., p. 44.
30. Kathleen Norris, *Hands Full of Living* (Amereon, 1998).
31. Sonny Carroll, *The Awakening*, www.waketolife.com

If you have enjoyed this book and would like to help us to send a copy of it and many other titles to needy pastors in the **Third World**, please write for further information or send your gift to:

Sovereign World Trust
PO Box 777, Tonbridge
Kent TN11 0ZS
United Kingdom

or to the **'Sovereign World'** distributor in your country.

Visit our website at **www.sovereign-world.org** for a full range of Sovereign World books.